OVERCOMING CORRUPTION

THE ESSENTIALS

OVERCOMING CORRUPTION

THE ESSENTIALS

Bertrand de Speville

DE SPEVILLE & ASSOCIATES

2010

TO ALL WHO LONG FOR
FREEDOM FROM CORRUPTION

First published in Great Britain 2010
de Speville & Associates
55 The Avenue, Richmond, Surrey, TW9 2AL
Produced by Michael Russell (Publishing) Ltd
Wilby Hall, Wilby, Norwich, NR16 2JP
in association with Waveney Typesetters
Wymondham, Norfolk
Printed in Great Britain
by the MPG Books Group
Bodmin and King's Lynn

ISBN 978-0-9564788-0-1

Contents

Foreword

If there is one person whom I admire for his sustained contribution to tackling corruption in societies across the world, it is Bertrand de Speville, the author of this down-to-earth practical book, written specially for high-level anticorruption decision makers in the cabinet rooms and the legislative chambers of the developed and the developing world.

This book is destined to become a standard work for those who, by virtue of their high political office, are assigned the unenviable task of developing national anticorruption policies. They will obviously need to have a grasp of the essentials in order to confront corruption decisively. This is where this book, written in language that is direct and concise, comes into its own.

It does not claim to be the last word on preventing the spread of corruption, about which much has been written by academic theoreticians and international institutional experts. Typically, the author chooses to offer his work instead as a modest 'briefing note' for those with responsibility for developing practical and effective policies to fight the scourge of corruption that impoverishes nations and retards orderly and sustainable social, economic and political growth in communities that need it most.

Fighting corruption has become a growth industry, and the proliferation of books on this subject is bewildering. Unfortunately, they are nothing more than interesting academic exercises and, from my standpoint, have little practical value for a busy decision maker or a legislator who wants to get straight to the heart of the matter.

This book lives up to its author's aim of helping those who

provide advice to governments on what it takes to get the job done well. Its appearance could not have been more timely as nations are shedding their natural ambivalence towards corrupt practices. They are showing greater determination to get to grips with a condition that they realise, from examples elsewhere, can be brought under control with a combination of strong political will, appropriate legal framework and public support.

I have for many years followed closely Bertrand de Speville's anticorruption strategies from the time he was appointed Commissioner of the Independent Commission Against Corruption of Hong Kong, where he made his mark as a thinking, pragmatic leader and maintained the Commission as the world's leading anticorruption outfit. The ICAC Hong Kong model is synonymous with high standards of professionalism and dedication that most other anticorruption organisations can only dream about.

This excellent book reveals a side of the man who today is a much respected and sought after international consultant; his highly developed sense of fairness and equity, even as he suggests tough measures to make corruption an unprofitable enterprise, speaks volumes for his personal integrity. He believes that much as we want to bring corruption under control, we must never let our passion and outrage get in the way of the rule of law.

He has shown us that there is no substitute for strict observance of the legal niceties in pursuing our anticorruption objectives. His legal training and subsequent distinguished career, culminating in his appointment as Solicitor General of Hong Kong prior to his heading the ICAC must have influenced the way he led a respected fighting organisation that carried out its difficult remit by showing the people of Hong Kong that there really was only one law for all.

In the years I have known Bertrand de Speville professionally, I have come to the honest conclusion many share with me that what he does not know about fighting corruption is not worth knowing.

Foreword

I commend this publication to all whose job it is to develop and implement national anticorruption policies and strategies. It will, no doubt, be equally useful to those who want to add to their knowledge on what it takes to get the job done.

TUNKU ABDUL AZIZ

Former Vice-Chairman, Transparency International
Former Special Adviser to the UN Secretary-General
on the Establishment of the UN Ethics Office

Preface

This little book is addressed to policymakers and legislators who have the responsibility of leading their country out of the mire of corruption. It is not an academic treatise on the causes and effects of corruption, about which a great deal has already been written. Nor is it a comprehensive textbook of the measures that might be applied in fighting corruption. Rather it is a briefing note for busy people who have to read on the run but who have to have a grasp of the essentials in order to set their country on the right road to success against the menace that undermines everything they are trying to build.

The book is also intended as an aide-mémoire for those who have been entrusted with the job of managing the implementation of the national anticorruption strategy. Even when the architecture is sound and the infrastructure has been built accordingly, there are many pitfalls to be avoided.

I hope that those who provide advice to governments will also find that this book adds to their store of knowledge on what it takes to get the job done.

I

A Glance at the Past

THE IMPORTANCE OF TACKLING CORRUPTION RECOGNISED

Corruption has not always been regarded by everyone as a bad thing. Until quite recently some respectable economists told us that in economic terms corruption could be a good thing. It is only about fifteen years since the world has recognised how destructive is the phenomenon we call 'corruption'.

Some say that this recognition began when the Soviet Union collapsed. After that, the West was no longer competing with the Communist Bloc for influence in non-aligned countries, many of which were plagued by corruption. After the fall of the Berlin Wall the provision of aid to developing countries and to countries in transition to democracy and free markets could be made conditional upon their undertaking reforms in governance, especially in tackling corruption.

Whether the demise of the Soviet Union was causal or coincidental, many nations appeared quite suddenly to take corruption seriously. International organisations, donor institutions and donor countries began giving the fight against corruption a priority it had never enjoyed before.

While the causes are still vigorously argued over, a general consensus on the effects quickly emerged – 'corruption threatens the rule of law, democracy and human rights, undermines good governance, fairness and social justice, distorts competition, hinders economic development and endangers the stability of democratic institutions and the moral foundations of society.'[1] A general awareness also developed of the links between corruption and organised crime, money laundering

1 From the Preamble to the Council of Europe's Criminal Law Convention on Corruption.

and terrorism. Bribery rather than brute force provides a safer and more effective method of serving the ends of serious criminality and terrorism.[2]

THE INTERNATIONAL DIMENSION

Since corruption like other criminality takes no account of national boundaries and since globalisation provides fresh opportunities for corrupt activities, states realised that an effective fight against corruption would require them to agree on common standards of enforcement and prevention and on arrangements for mutual judicial assistance in investigating and prosecuting corruption offences and in recovering the proceeds.

Regional initiatives resulted in the adoption of a number of international instruments specifically aimed at combating corruption. The Organisation of American States led the way. In 1997 its InterAmerican Convention Against Corruption came into force. Also in 1997 came the Council of Europe's Twenty Guiding Principles for the Fight against Corruption which 'identifies the areas in which state action is necessary for a comprehensive and efficient strategy against corruption'. In May 1998 the Council of Europe's Council of Ministers authorised the setting up of the 'Group of States against Corruption' (GRECO) whose object is to develop states' compliance with their undertakings in the fight against corruption through 'mutual evaluation and peer pressure'. The same year the Council of Europe adopted the Criminal Law Convention on Corruption and, the following year, the Civil Law Convention on Corruption. The year 2000 saw the Council's promulgation of the Model Code of Conduct for Public Officials. The OECD's Convention on Combating Bribery of Foreign Public

2 Michael Hershman, member of the International Group of Experts on Corruption, on the link between terrorism and corruption: 'The bomb that killed over 100 people in the Moscow theatre was carried on a bus from Grozny. It was stopped 50 times at roadblocks, and in every case a bribe was paid and no checks were carried out.'

Officials in International Business Transactions came into force in 1999. In Africa the Southern African Development Community adopted the Protocol against Corruption in 2001 The African Union's heads of state summit in 2003 adopted its Convention on Preventing and Combating Corruption and related offences. In 2005 the member states of the Asia-Pacific Economic Cooperation established the Anti-Corruption Taskforce which has since produced several anticorruption documents. In December 2005 the United Nations Convention Against Corruption entered into force and 143 member states are now parties to the convention.

NUMEROUS ATTEMPTS, FEW SUCCESSES

Although it is only in the last decade of the twentieth century that corruption has been so prominent on the agendas of national governments and international institutions, the destructive effects of the phenomenon were realised long before. At least from the nineteenth century the criminal laws of all modern states have made bribery and related conduct serious offences. As corruption grew and spread, states reacted in the traditional way of dealing with antisocial behaviour: they passed more criminal laws and introduced heavier penalties. The answer was thought to lie in repression and deterrence. In some countries special investigation units were created, usually within the police force, to deal specifically with cases of corruption. Nowhere however did the policy of repression and deterrence appear to make any impact on the problem: almost everywhere corruption continued to grow, especially in developing countries. The law enforcement agencies themselves became corrupted to the point where they could no longer be trusted to enforce the laws. The special units within the police proved useless. Citizens no longer trusted the police, prosecutors and judges to deal with cases of corruption. On every continent corruption gnawed at or undermined everything that nation states were trying to build. In many countries people came to regard corruption as a fact of life, to be endured and accommodated. Some even came to think of corruption as part of their culture, a state of affairs incapable of change.

In this worsening climate one or two rays of hope nevertheless pierced the gloom. In Singapore the situation had become so serious in the years immediately following the Second World War that the British authorities created in 1952 a Corrupt Practices Investigation Bureau. It had little effect until in 1959 Singapore gained its independence under the leadership of Prime Minister Lee Kwan Yew. His personal intolerance of corruption galvanised the people of Singapore. The CPIB was placed under his direct control and before long was making a marked impact.

Hong Kong by the 1960s was regarded as one of the most corruption-ridden places anywhere. The Anti-Corruption Unit, formed within the Royal Hong Kong Police, was having no effect. The disappearance from Hong Kong of a senior police officer under investigation by that unit for serious corruption resulted in the establishment by law of the Independent Commission Against Corruption. Its role was, and continues to be, to lead the implementation of Hong Kong's strategy against the affliction.

In both Singapore and Hong Kong, places that had long been regarded as synonymous with corruption, profound change gradually occurred. Within a generation they both came to be regarded as relatively corruption-free. In Hong Kong even the businessmen came to acknowledge that they could not have built Hong Kong into the international metropolis it became if the corruption of the 1950s and '60s had continued. How was it done? If it was done there, could it be done elsewhere?

In several countries attempts were made in the 1980s to fight corruption simply by creating a more or less independent body to do the job. These bodies had mixed fortunes. Some were partly successful, most were failures whose efforts at tackling corruption foundered. With hindsight the reasons for failure have become clear. Likewise the reasons for the rare successes.

2

The Seven Essentials of Fighting Corruption

CONTEXT

The modern world has come to realise that ethical values, integrity and good governance are the foundations of a successful state. The world has also come to realise that corruption undermines those foundations. When the foundations are undermined, what is then likely to follow is collapse – collapse of the rule of law, collapse of the economic and political systems, collapse of social development, collapse of security and rage at the loss of the ethical underpinnings of our lives. It is hardly surprising that the fight against the scourge of corruption has become vital

In recent years the international donor community, led by the World Bank, has come to take a prominent role in advising the world on how to fight corruption. The Bank, followed by the rest of the donor community, has taken a conscious decision to put fighting corruption high on its agenda. The Bank was and is well placed to do so because that institution has profound influence on the development of our world and because it is one of the largest distributors of economic and technical aid. However, the experience of the international donors in fighting corruption is limited and patchy, and the results have not been impressive. As the Bank's 2007 policy paper 'Strengthening World Bank Group Engagement in Governance and Anticorruption' says: 'The growing attention to these issues has yet to result in the major improvements worldwide that everyone would like to see. Some countries have improved, but others have deteriorated, and the world on average has not made sufficient progress on governance and corruption control.'[1] Some in the Bank would say there have not yet been any 'discernible improvements'.[2] Many outside the Bank would say things have not merely stagnated but got worse.

What has gone wrong? Why has progress been negligible despite the time, effort and resources spent on the problem? What seems largely to have happened is the conflation of good governance with anticorruption and the attempt to deal with corruption by governance reforms. As the Bank itself asserted: 'Corruption is a governance issue, and can be addressed by the Bank within the framework established for governance.'[3]

The Bank makes the point that governance and anticorruption are not the same thing.[4] In practice, however, it has failed to distinguish between them. Corruption is the disease that attacks governance. But if corruption is the disease, why do we suppose that governance measures of themselves will cure it? Does the disease not have to be treated with specific remedies if governance is to be restored to health? Unless corruption is attacked effectively, governance is undermined and governance reforms fail to take root. That does not mean that governance reforms have to wait until corruption is overcome. Anticorruption and governance reforms are interdependent. They can and should run in parallel. They are complementary and should be advanced together. The terrible error has been the belief that getting governance right would dispose of corruption, that blanket governance reform would stifle corruption.

Belatedly the world is beginning to realise that a sharper, more focused approach to fighting corruption is necessary.

1 The phrase 'has not made sufficient progress' read in an earlier draft 'has almost stagnated'.

2 See August 2006 draft of the GAC paper.

3 1997 report 'Helping Countries Combat Corruption – The Role of the World Bank', ch 1: 'Key Messages'.

4 '10 Myths About Governance and Corruption' – Daniel Kaufmann, Director of the World Bank Institute, 2005.

Policy makers in those countries hampered by corruption are looking for an effective way of dealing with the problem.

THE NECESSARY ELEMENTS

Political leaders are worried by the growth of corruption. They see the consequences and they realise that things can only get worse if effective action is not taken quickly. It is little comfort to the people of a country to know that theirs is not the only country to be thus afflicted, nor that their situation is nowhere near the worst. Each country has its unique characteristics and its corruption, no doubt, has some special features. However, corruption is a universal phenomenon – no country is devoid of it – and, despite its numerous manifestations, it has certain features wherever it appears. It is now widely recognised that combating corruption successfully in any country requires certain conditions. These are the seven essentials:

Will There must exist the political will to act against the problem. Political will on tackling corruption is usually fragile and short-lived. From the beginning everything must be done to nurture it.

Law There must be strong laws comprising clear offences that reflect the values of the community, effective powers of investigation and rules of evidence that assist the proper prosecution of those charged with corruption offences.

Strategy Fighting corruption requires a clear, complete and coherent strategy, and the strategy must include three elements:

effective enforcement of the laws;

prevention of corruption by eliminating from systems, large and small, the opportunities for corruption;

educating the public about corruption and persuading people to help fight it.

Coordinated action To be effective, the implementation of these elements must be coordinated. So far, coordination resulting in success against corruption has been achieved only by a specialised anticorruption body.

Resources National leaders must recognise that fighting corruption successfully requires resources, human and financial.

Public support The authorities cannot fight the problem without the help of the people. Therefore the community must be actively involved from the beginning.

Endurance Everyone must realise that beating corruption will take time and may cause pain. And that, once the problem has been brought under control, it must be kept under control. In consequence the commitment must be long-term, which means that the provision of adequate resources for the fight becomes a permanent item of annual national expenditure.

THE STRATEGY ITSELF

The objective of the strategy in each country is to reduce corruption to the point where, first, it no longer undermines what people are trying to build in their own country and, second, the people will see corruption for the destructive menace that it is and guard against it.

As for the strategy itself, it is self-evident that one of its elements has to be the effective enforcement of the national laws against corruption. It must be recognised, however, that enforcement of the laws alone never brings corruption under control. That lesson has been learned many times in different countries that have tried to deal with a growing problem by making and enforcing harsher laws, only to find that the problem gets worse. Prosecution and conviction do not in themselves provide a solution. While it is essential that there should be effective action in making corruption a crime that carries a high risk of being caught, convicted and punished, it is now generally recognised that there are two other elements equally essential to success: prevention, and public education and support. They are the product of two common-sensical thoughts.

The first is that all of us live and work in and with systems – systems large and small. As members of an orderly society we create them and function within them. These systems present us with the opportunities to take improper advantage of them. We are only human; sooner or later some of us will yield to the temptation presented by the system we work in. It is rightly said that a system is only as good as the people who make it work. But the converse is equally true: people are only as good as the systems they have to work with. If a system is bad because it offers opportunities for corruption, the people who operate the system are likely themselves to become bad. It makes sense, therefore, to examine each of these systems, large or small, and make changes to it as necessary, or even replace the system or abolish it altogether, so as to eliminate the opportunities for corruption that currently exist within it.

The second line of thought concerns people – all of us in the community. If we are to turn against corruption, we must first learn about corruption – what it does to our community, how it spreads like dry rot. Then we have to realise that it can be beaten, but only if each of us is ready to play our part. Finally, we must shun corruption and determine that we will not allow it to be part of our daily lives, as it is now in so many countries. So, for the whole community there must be education and there must be developed the willingness to help in the fight.

People, however, have an ambivalent attitude to corruption – an attitude of uncertainty compounded by tolerance, indifference or resignation, a feeling that corruption is so pervasive that nothing can be done about it and we might as well learn to live with it. There seems little point in helping the authorities to combat corruption – especially if they themselves are believed to be corrupt!

That attitude must be changed for two reasons. First, if the laws against corruption are to be enforced, the allegations and suspicions of corruption have to be investigated. But, corruption being secretive and complicitous, there is nothing to investigate unless those who know that something is going on are prepared to say so. It is very difficult to develop the willingness to help in this way, especially in countries where denunciation to the authorities is anathema or where the authorities are deeply distrusted. Yet it must be done, for unless the authorities are given good information about what is happening, they will be powerless to do anything. People must therefore be brought to feel that corruption has to be resisted, that the information they have is essential in the fight and that in giving information they will be protected and respected.

The second reason why people's attitude to corruption must change is the practical recognition that in the long term success can come only with the development of intolerance of corruption in the hearts and minds of every one of us. The effectiveness of enforcement is limited – you can investigate and prosecute for ever but, without a change of attitude throughout the community, enforcement will not overcome corruption. Eliminating the opportunities for corruption is limited – you can go on improving the systems for ever but, without a change of heart and mind in the people who operate the systems, the corrupt will always find a way round them.

These three elements of the strategy – enforcement, prevention and education – must move forward together and complement each other; for when they are made interdependent, any success in one of them enhances the other two. Now the strategy is more powerful than the sum of its parts – truly an effective weapon.

THE MECHANISM FOR IMPLEMENTING THE STRATEGY

If it is decided that the three arms of the strategy must move forward together and complement each other, it follows that their implementation will have to be coordinated by a body or person. In many countries a special body has been created, or will be created, to perform that coordinating role. If coordination is to be effective, that anticorruption body needs the power to direct the action to be taken. Being countries governed in accordance with the rule of law, their people will insist that any powers granted to the coordinating body should be specified by law.

Implementing each of the arms of the strategy requires distinct skills, skills not usually found in a single individual. The investigator is unlikely also to be an educator or a systems analyst. No doubt specialised people are to be found in existing agencies of government in all countries. So, one of the ways of implementing each arm of the strategy would be to make that arm the job of an existing agency or unit of government. That agency or unit should be part of the public administration, as opposed to a non-governmental organisation, so that it can be properly kept under control and made properly accountable.

If an existing government agency has the capacity to undertake the implementation of one of the arms of the strategy and can be trusted to do the job properly, it may be better to use that agency than to create a new implementing agency. If, for example, the investigation of corruption allegations can safely be left in the hands of the police, it may be decided to leave investigation to the police. If however there is reason to doubt the ability or integrity of the police, it may be necessary to form an investigating unit separate from the police and to make it part of the anticorruption body. It would also avoid the situation in which police officers responsible for investigating corruption have a dual system of accountability, namely accountability to the head of the police for administrative and personnel matters and operational accountability to the anti-corruption body. This is a matter that the leadership of the various countries will decide but, if the police are widely believed to be corrupt, a new and separate unit will have to be formed, at least so far as investigation is concerned.

The same reasoning applies for the two other arms of the strategy. If an existing agency can be given the responsibility and can be made operationally answerable to the anti-corruption coordinating body, that may be the better way to proceed. But existing agencies have their own portfolio of responsibilities which must take priority. Is it realistic to expect them to make fighting corruption their top priority at the expense of their main responsibility?

All the details of implementing each arm of the strategy need not, indeed should not, be decided at the beginning. As

Martin Luther King once said: 'You don't have to see the whole staircase ... just take the first step.' It is unnecessary to decide at the outset exactly how the anticorruption message will be conveyed to police recruits, nor whether the promotion system in the public administration should be the first system to be examined. It is the strategy and the institutional mechanism for putting it into practice that should be decided at this stage.

STEPS FOR THE ADOPTION OF THE STRATEGY

The campaign against corruption should be built step by step:

1. Adopting the strategy and the institutional mechanism by which it will be implemented.
2. Raising public awareness and understanding of the government's determination to deal with corruption.
3. Deciding the main policy issues that will affect the course of the campaign.
4. Making a survey of the current state of affairs and of public attitudes to corruption so as to provide a benchmark against which to measure future progress.
5. Preparing and enacting the legislation that will state the strategy, create its implementing mechanism, grant the necessary powers and provide the safeguards against abuse.
6. Appointing the coordinating body and providing financial and technical support that will be needed at the outset.
7. Selecting and training the personnel who will be given the responsibility for carrying out the coordinating body's instructions.
8. The start of operations by the coordinator.
9. Developing the campaign over time.
10. Accounting regularly for the conduct and progress of the campaign.

It is important that consensus for the struggle should be built at each stage in ever- widening circles, so that before long the consensus becomes nationwide.

PRIORITIES UNDER EACH ARM OF THE STRATEGY

Each arm of the strategy – enforcement, prevention and education – is equally important to the success of the campaign. They must advance together, work together and support each other. However, it has to be recognised that for the public it is the enforcement arm that will provide evidence that the government means what it says. The evidence will have to appear reasonably quickly for there to be any chance of convincing a sceptical public. Therefore the coordinating body's priority task should be to get the investigating unit operational by the time the government launches the campaign. Then, in quick succession, the coordinating body will want to get the prevention and public education teams moving.

Priorities are of two kinds – organisational and operational. Having just considered organisational priorities, it is necessary to say something about operational priorities because an important policy issue arises in connection with investigations. While it is perhaps obvious that, in relation to prevention and public education, those tasks that are regarded as the most pressing or the most likely to succeed should be undertaken first, it does not follow that the most serious allegations of corruption should be given investigative priority at the expense of minor matters. It is very important that every allegation should be quickly and properly investigated, no matter how insignificant it may seem to be. The reasons are these:

1. What appears to be a minor matter quite often unravels into a much more serious case.
2. For the citizen who has brought himself to make a complaint, the matter will be important. If it is dismissed as unimportant, he is unlikely ever to return to the authorities, perhaps with a crucial piece of information.

If community support is to be won, the minor complaint must be taken seriously.

3 Picking and choosing which reports to investigate and which to ignore gives rise to suspicion of improper influence having affected the decision or, worse, of corruption in the investigating unit.

4 Ignoring some complaints gives the impression that some corruption is tolerated, that double standards apply.

5 The fact is that widespread small-scale corruption does serious damage to the wellbeing of a country. Furthermore, a single small act of corruption can have catastrophic consequences; instances come readily to mind in the field of security or public health.

The consequence of adopting a policy of investigating all reports capable of investigation is that the investigating arm of the coordinating body is demand led; its workload will depend on the number of reports received. Furthermore, investigating corruption is labour intensive. These two factors have implications for resource requirements and inevitably the agency needs more investigators than preventors and educators.

Of course, the amount of resources put into investigating what is indeed a minor matter will be small in comparison to the resources put into investigating a major matter. What is important is that in both cases the public should feel the investigation has been properly done. And in that connection the community can have an important role to play.

THE COMMUNITY'S ROLE IN CLOSING INVESTIGATIONS

Every day the headlines tell us 'Corruption Here' 'Corruption There'. It is not surprising we come to believe corruption is everywhere. Allegations of corruption fly around but never seem to be resolved. Nobody is charged, let alone convicted. We never know if the matter has been properly investigated. These allegations just accumulate, polluting the atmosphere. Before long we believe all our public figures, all our politicians and public officials, indeed all those around us are corrupt. This state of mind is not peculiar to any one country – it occurs in every country where people believe that allegations of corruption are not properly investigated. We are obviously in need of fresh air.

One of the functions of an anticorruption body is to investigate thoroughly the corruption allegations that are made to it. And the public has to be satisfied about that. People have to be reassured that the anticorruption body has done a proper job of investigation. Experience in places like Hong Kong, Singapore and Botswana shows us that most allegations or suspicions of corruption do not result in a prosecution in court. The reason is usually that the necessary evidence is lacking or even that the allegation was mistaken. The investigation can go no further and must therefore be closed, but not before we are satisfied it really has been properly investigated.

How can the anticorruption body reassure the public about that? It would be disastrous to make available for public scrutiny all those investigations that have to be closed. It would wreck the confidentiality of the anticorruption body. Some of the anticorruption body's work must be confidential: the public expects it.

There is a solution. It has been used successfully in Hong Kong over many years. A committee of trustworthy citizens is given the role of looking at investigations that investigators propose should be closed and of advising whether or not the investigation should be closed. These citizens meet about once a month for half a day and consider the cases that are to be closed. They can question the investigating officers. If they agree with the proposed closure, they advise accordingly. If they do not, they can advise that further investigation should be done or that the legal advice should be reconsidered. Their work is of course confidential.

In that way the people are reassured that ordinary citizens, acting in the public interest and on behalf of the public, have satisfied themselves that investigations have been thoroughly done and can properly be closed. If that committee is satisfied, the public can be too. The air begins to clear.

SOME PRACTICAL POLICY QUESTIONS

In carrying out the anticorruption strategy, a number of policy issues arise. They should be decided well before the start of operations so that they can be incorporated into standing operating procedures. Some have resource implications and for that reason need government endorsement. A few of them are described here.

Investigating policy The crucial question of investigating policy has already been mentioned. It bears repeating: investigate all complaints of corruption capable of being investigated; conversely, do not initiate investigations but be responsive to the community's concerns.

An anticorruption body made responsible for investigating complaints of corruption must also be able to investigate other forms of criminality suspected of being connected to or facilitated by corruption. It is often the only way of getting to the underlying corruption.

Openness and confidentiality Developing the support of the public requires first the development of its trust. People need to know enough about the anticorruption body's activities to feel confident that it is doing a good job and not misusing its powers. At the same time people must be able to trust the agency with confidential information and feel that their identity will not be revealed without their consent. People not only understand but expect that some of the anticorruption body's work must be confidential.

In an open, democratic society it is therefore essential to winning and retaining public support that an anticorruption body should have a guiding policy that it acts openly and transparently in all it does except in those areas of its work that need to be confidential.

To what extent should the conduct of the campaign against

corruption be open and transparent? There are some aspects that should, at least for a time and sometimes indefinitely, be kept confidential. When an allegation of corruption is made to the agency about any citizen, especially a member of the legislature or a prominent businessman, publicising the allegation can damage the reputation of that citizen. More importantly, allowing it to be known that an allegation has been made and that an investigation must therefore be underway is likely to frustrate the investigation by allowing the suspects to cover their traces. A balance must be struck between freedom of expression and the public's right to access to information on one hand and the public interest in the effective investigation of corruption and the protection of reputations from unwarranted accusation on the other.

In accordance with the guiding principle of an anticorruption body that openness and transparency are to prevail except where the public interest requires confidentiality, the general rule should be as follows: the work of educating the public and developing community support is never confidential; the work of corruption prevention by systems enhancement is sometimes confidential depending on the necessary requirements of the 'client' department for whom the prevention advice is provided; and the work of investigating allegations or suspicions of corruption is always confidential.

The division of labour As regards the investigation of corruption offences by an anticorruption body, the jurisdiction of the police to investigate all criminality including corruption should not be altered. As a matter of law the police should continue to be able to investigate corruption. The public should be able to choose to report allegations of corruption to the police or to the anticorruption body.

However, an administrative direction to all departments, authorities and agencies of the public administration should require them to refer all reports or suspicions of corruption, uninvestigated, to the specialised body established for the purpose of dealing with corruption. For its part the body would refer all non-corruption matters to other agencies as appropriate. Criminal matters not involving corruption would be referred to the police and the police would be expected, but not obliged, to refer corruption matters to the anticorruption body. However, when allegations of corruption concern police officers, the police should be obliged to refer them to the anti-corruption body.

As regards prosecution of corruption offences, it is a valuable safeguard against oppressive prosecution that the distinction between investigating and prosecuting should be maintained and that those functions should be carried out by separate bodies. The anticorruption body should investigate, the public prosecutor should prosecute.

3
Political Will: How Can It Be Developed and Sustained?

SETTING THE SCENE

A typical picture – the country has been mired in corruption for years. People have grown sick of it. The elections have seen off the old governing party and the opposition now finds itself in power, having promised that it will deal with corruption. The little flame of anticorruption fervour burns bright. Yet all who have worked in the field know how short-lived it can be. The slightest political draught can blow it out. There is a brief window of opportunity, sometimes little more than a few weeks, to help build up that fragile political will for long enough to put in place a sound national anticorruption strategy and the means of putting it into effect.

Our political leaders very rarely know how to tackle corruption. Why should we expect them to be knowledgeable in the subject? But in the short period before they put the corruption problem into the 'too difficult' basket, they are prepared to listen to good advice.

The national leader, or more likely one of his ministers, has before him one of the better advisers of the donor community. The adviser realises that the political will to tackle corruption is likely to be short-lived if he cannot persuade the minister about certain matters. Here are the four things the adviser should be ready to convey, quickly, clearly and concisely:

1. Devising a national strategy that makes sense and a method of implementing it effectively that is feasible.
2. Bringing the cabinet along from the outset.

3 Developing public support from the outset.
4 Dealing with the past.

For the time being, let us put the first matter to one side – it is the subject of a later chapter. Let us assume for the moment that the adviser has sketched out the strategy and its implementation and that the minister stands duly persuaded. Let us turn to the remaining three matters, matters that are quite distinct from each other but are closely connected.

CABINET CONSENSUS

We have often seen a government's anticorruption champion come to grief. The reason is usually his failure to appreciate the need to take his cabinet colleagues along. If he charges off on his own, he will quickly find he is alone and unsupported. If, out of the blue, he suddenly presents them with detailed plans and budgets, the reaction from some of his cabinet colleagues, especially those who are not particularly enthusiastic about the cause, is to find some reason to defer the matter. The finance minister may well say it is the first he has heard of this proposed expenditure. It is therefore vital that the champion should get his colleagues to sign up. Their approval in principle is needed. A short cabinet policy paper should seek approval of and for the following:

1 A national strategy that consists of enforcement, prevention and education in combination.
2 An institutional mechanism that will be responsible for leading the implementation of the strategy.
3 The necessity for public support.
4 The commitment to allocate adequate resources.
5 An issues consultation of the opinion-formers of the community.
6 The need to consider the past.

Approval provides the green light. Non-approval may identify the opposition and its reasons and provides the opportunity for reconsideration.

This cabinet approval is needed at the outset. Unfortunately the necessity to obtain it is often overlooked. Once it is obtained and when the consent to an issues consultation is given, it is time to carry out the consultation and begin work on a detailed implementation paper for the cabinet's later consideration. The implementation paper should include findings from the consultation so as to show the extent of public support for the implementation proposals.

PUBLIC SUPPORT

Although our leaders are there to lead, none of them likes to get too far ahead of public opinion. Our leaders draw strength from public support. It is only prudent for them to test the wind and at the same time to give the lead. Consulting the public is a tried and tested method of achieving both objectives. The public should be consulted about the most important issues that arise in tackling corruption. How could they be conveyed? A consultation paper would set out each of these issues and invite a response. Since it is not possible to consult everyone, it is the opinion-formers of the community who should be consulted, those who shape public opinion in every sector of the community.

The consultation paper would serve several purposes. First, it would provide information about the main issues involved in fighting corruption and what the government is considering. Second, it would seek the views of individuals and representative organisations from all sectors of the community and would thus give an indication of what opinion-formers thought about these various issues. Third, the responses would be likely to reassure the more prudent members of the government that it was not moving too far ahead of the community. Fourth, opinion-formers would be pleased to be asked and given the opportunity to 'buy into' the anticorruption drive. Finally, the responses would enable the government to gauge public support for each of the various ideas in the paper and allow it to develop its operational strategy for tackling corruption in the light of the responses.

The consultation is not conducted as a national survey of attitude to or perception of corruption, but rather as a sounding that gives a clear indication of the views and suggestions of the leaders of opinion at all levels of the community. The sample is chosen in consultation with three or four community institutions so as to ensure that the list of consultees is fairly balanced.

Ten main categories of organisations and individuals should be consulted: political leaders, the public and private sectors, the media, employer and employee organisations, educators and other professions, community-based organisations and religious organisations. The political leaders category could be divided into subcategories of national politicians and local leaders; the educational category would contain primary, secondary and tertiary subcategories; the business category could be subdivided into, for example, the extractive industries, other enterprises, trade associations and financial services. Public servants would be split into general administrators, judiciary, police and other disciplined services. Community organisations might comprise village councils, women's groups, youth organisations and a general subcategory.

The consultation document sets out an explanation of each issue, a dozen or so. Each explanation is followed by specific questions, a total of 30–40 questions. In some of the questions respondents are invited to explain the reason for their choice or to propose their own solution. One of those issues might be how to deal with the past.

The document (in more than one language if necessary) is sent throughout the country via the postal service or the administrative network. Consultees are given a certain time to respond if they wish and are assured of confidentiality. Publicity shortly beforehand can make all the difference to the response rate.

The replies contained in each response are recorded and analysed. The analysis allows a comparison of the responses of the different categories to each question, as well as a comparison of the subcategories and the main category. As mentioned earlier, the responses inform the strategy implementation paper that should be considered by the cabinet soon after the consultation has been completed.

DEALING WITH THE PAST – MAKING A FRESH START

The past is likely to cause an anticorruption initiative to fail, in two ways. Those who realise they are at risk from an effective drive against corruption will do what they can to ensure that it never flies. At an earlier stage, as our leaders contemplate the realities of effective action, they themselves may feel their anticorruption fervour fading. The thought that such action may affect political allies and colleagues, perhaps even friends and family, has a dampening effect. It may extinguish the initiative completely.

Time and again experience shows us that a new initiative against corruption can be destroyed by the past. So at the outset the leadership of the country should consider how the past is to be dealt with. It may be desirable, if not essential, that the initiative should make a fresh start, should break with the past and signal a change of climate. That would mean overlooking or somehow accommodating past conduct. There are moral, practical and political justifications for such a course.

First, if new rules are to apply and a new climate of enforcement is to prevail, by which standards should past conduct be measured? In a new climate under changed rules and different expectations it is perhaps not right that acts done in a different moral climate should be judged by these new standards.

Second, public awareness and expectation that something effective might at last be done about corruption is likely to result in a spate of allegations, some of which will go back a long way. From a pragmatic point of view, there is a real danger that a new anticorruption authority will be overwhelmed by numerous allegations of matters going back years, that it will simply not be able to cope with the volume. Can the country risk its fresh initiative against corruption being swamped by old matters, of its newly launched anticorruption authority sinking under the weight of past misdeeds? For the reasons explained later, it is not an option for the anticorruption authority merely to refuse to investigate these allegations.

Third, attempting to deal with old matters uses up resources and restricts the capacity to investigate allegations of new corruption. Would it not be preferable to use available resources to address the present and the future?

Fourth, as already mentioned, the political will to defeat corruption is liable to be undermined by those in positions of influence who could be adversely affected by effective action against the problem. That reality should be weighed in assessing the risk and consequences of the anticorruption initiative failing.

This is a delicate and difficult political matter, to be decided at the highest level. But it should be decided at the outset. If the decision is delayed, the success of the campaign against corruption is put at risk.

The options are limited:

1 Declare an 'amnesty' to the effect that matters occurring before a certain date will not be investigated.
2 Initiate a 'truth and reconciliation' process by which those coming forward within a certain time and publicly admitting their past acts of corruption will not be prosecuted.
3 Restrict the use of new powers of investigation to investigating matters occurring after a certain date.
4 Rely on the legal principle that 'new' offences do not apply retrospectively.
5 Limit the number of investigations by selecting what to investigate.
6 Do nothing in the hope that all allegations can be investigated to the satisfaction of the public.

Before considering each of these options further, the reasons why it would be unwise to allow the anticorruption authority itself to choose not to investigate certain allegations should be explained. Corruption cannot be beaten without public support. The public will support the anticorruption authority only if the authority gains its trust and confidence. The authority's investigation policy is essential to winning that trust and confidence. It is most important that the authority should aim to investigate every pursuable report of corruption. There are five good reasons for adopting such a policy. They were set out in chapter 2 but merit being repeated.

First, putting aside even a minor allegation will deter the complainant from returning, perhaps with a much more important matter. Second, what appears minor quite often turns out to be serious when investigated. Third, numerous small acts of corruption are harmful to a country's wellbeing, and a single small act of corruption can have catastrophic consequences. Fourth, it is not right that the anticorruption authority should give the impression that only some corruption matters, that double standards apply. Finally, picking and choosing what to investigate and what not to investigate raises suspicions of improper motives, if not of actual corruption. People will not understand why some allegations are investigated and some are not. They will mistrust the authority and lose confidence in it.

A policy of investigating all reports capable of investigation means that the authority does not pick and choose. As regards allegations from the past, the agency will attract public mistrust if the decision whether or not to investigate very serious cases that come to light is left to the agency itself. That is why that decision must be taken elsewhere. Let us now turn to each of the options for dealing with the past.

I DRAWING A LINE UNDER THE PAST

Making a fresh start by declaring that matters occurring before a certain date will not be investigated requires a legal provision to that effect. If the moral and pragmatic justifications referred to earlier are to apply, the date it takes effect should be when the new law comes into force or when the authority becomes operational.

If conduct occurring before a certain date is not to be investigated, should the anticorruption authority nevertheless be allowed to investigate a matter so serious that it cannot be overlooked, regardless of when it occurred? Should certain extremely serious conduct be investigated no matter when it took place? If so, how is it to be determined whether the conduct is sufficiently serious? Presumably investigations already started would continue, or at any rate those investigations where the suspect had been interviewed or had fled the jurisdiction.

If there is to be such an exception to the amnesty, what would be needed is a mechanism for deciding whether a matter that occurred before the operative date is so serious that it must be investigated. This too is a delicate matter, but a few parameters can be stated. First, the person or persons making the decision must command public trust. Second, the decision must be made independently of the anticorruption authority itself. The decision could be seen to have political overtones from which the authority should be kept at a safe distance. Third, the decision must be treated as final.

The mechanism for making that determination would have to be such as to reassure the public that the decision was being properly taken by people it could trust. It could be a small committee of three prominent persons of integrity, selected perhaps from a group comprising the head of the judiciary, the leader of the legislature, the controller and auditor of public expenditure, a religious leader and a leader from the private sector or civil society.

The function of the committee would be to certify that an alleged or suspected corruption offence was or was not sufficiently serious to warrant action being taken under the law against corruption. The allegation would be put before the committee by the head of the anticorruption authority where he felt that it might fall within this exception to the amnesty. He would then act in accordance with its decision – either investigate the matter or close the file.

Such an exception allows very serious matters to be investigated and helps to make the notion of amnesty more palatable.

2 PUBLIC ADMISSION OF CORRUPT CONDUCT

A process of 'truth and reconciliation' would require a public admission in exchange for immunity from prosecution. Anything less than immunity would be unlikely to attract an admission. There are difficulties with this option. While a truth and reconciliation process has value in cases of human rights abuse, the notion of reconciliation sits strangely in corruption cases where there are usually no identifiable victims of the offence with whom to be reconciled. Furthermore, public forgiveness without restitution of the proceeds of the corruption would probably be unacceptable to the community. But it is equally improbable that the corrupt would be prepared to surrender their gains. They are more likely to believe that there will continue to be minimal risk of being effectively investigated and prosecuted. For these reasons this option is unlikely to succeed.

3 RESTRICTING THE USE OF INVESTIGATIVE POWERS

This option would require a legal provision preventing the use of the investigative powers contained in the new law from being used to investigate matters occurring before a certain date or, conversely, allowing the powers to be used to investigate matters occurring only after a certain date, that date being presumably the date the law comes into force. The difficulty with this option is the ambivalence of its moral stance. The public will be unable to see why the powers can be used in some cases but not in others. That will lead to public mistrust and loss of confidence.

4 RELY ON THE LEGAL PRINCIPLE THAT 'NEW' OFFENCES DO NOT APPLY RETROSPECTIVELY

The difficulty with this option is that very often the offences in the new law are not themselves new but merely restatements of offences that have long been part of the criminal law. The public will see no difference between the old and the new nor understand why 'new' conduct can be prosecuted but 'old' conduct cannot.

5 LIMIT NUMBER OF INVESTIGATIONS BY SELECTION

For the reasons set out earlier, the anticorruption authority must not be selective in what it does and does not investigate. This option should therefore be rejected as posing the greatest risk to the success of the anticorruption initiative.

6 DOING NOTHING

This option has the merit of avoiding a difficult decision that carries considerable political risk. The question is whether that risk is outweighed by the risk of the anticorruption initiative failing through the withering of political will or the overwhelming practical effect of the past.

People need to be given time to consider the dilemma if they are to accept the notion of an amnesty. If the first option is to be adopted, it would be imperative that the ground be carefully prepared. The fight against corruption cannot be won without the support of the public. If this is to be retained, people need to understand the reasons why an amnesty is necessary to enable the country to break out of its web of corruption and move on. And if it is true that people of all walks of life and of all ranks of society have been tainted by the corruption of the past, the realisation than the amnesty would apply to people of every rank and occupation would be salutary.

CONCLUDING REMARKS

Political will to fight corruption is as easily extinguished as a candle flame. It needs protecting and encouraging. Advisers can help by suggesting to a country's leadership what practical steps could be taken at the outset. International and bilateral donors are often well positioned to help.

The government's anticorruption champion needs protection from and by his ministerial colleagues. That is why their endorsement in principle for the way forward is essential. The expression of community endorsement encourages the government and provides another mantle of protection for that little flame. The threat of the past is a reality that has to be faced. Therefore the idea of amnesty has to be thought about rationally. The public should be given the opportunity to do that and express its view. The issues consultation of opinion-formers provides the opportunity.

We know how fragile is the political will to fight corruption. It is the first essential for success. Without it, nothing can be achieved. Everything must therefore be done to protect and reinforce it. The three practical steps described here – cabinet consensus, community endorsement and dealing with the past – have each been tried and tested.

Once established, the institutional mechanism for taking forward the anticorruption strategy becomes responsible for developing public support. It is that growing public support that will strengthen and sustain the political will essential for the long, costly and painful struggle to success against corruption.

4
Our Values in the Law – Criminal, Administrative and Civil

INTRODUCTION

A community tackles corruption because it wants to uphold the values it has on this age-old problem, values that in so many countries have been undermined, neglected and buried in the rush to riches. In recent years the world has come to realise the harm done by this neglect. Most countries are now trying to resurrect those values. It is worth reminding ourselves that, if governance is about how things are run, tackling corruption is about upholding certain values. Governance and anticorruption are not at all the same thing.

As is the case with the most important norms of social conduct, it is in the criminal law of any modern state that the core values on corruption are to be found. Those core values should be clearly and simply stated so that the law can be understood and applied. The community's values set out in the law is the second of the seven essentials needed in any country if corruption is to be overcome and controlled.

CORE VALUES IN CRIMINAL LAW

'Corruption' is a wide term with many meanings. Much ink has been spilled in trying to define it for the purpose of devising a national anticorruption strategy. No more will be spilled here except to provide a generic description of the antisocial conduct proscribed in all our penal codes under the heading 'Corruption Offences'. Under this heading our laws criminalise the unauthorised trading of entrusted authority.

A few points should be made about this description. First, it presupposes that the individual has been entrusted by his employer or principal or by the community with some authority to act. Second, that the individual has traded that authority with someone else, namely, he has used his authority in exchange for some material benefit. Third, that the individual acted in that way without the approval of his employer or principal or the community. Fourth, this description applies to conduct in any part of the community; it is not limited to the public sector. Fifth, a trade implies two parties, so the description embraces the conduct of each of the parties, the giver and the receiver.

Bribery At the heart of all our criminal laws on corruption lies the offence of bribery. Modern laws usually distinguish between public sector bribery (where at least of one of the parties is a public official) and non-public sector bribery (where neither party is a public official). Some countries still criminalise only public sector corruption but that situation is changing as countries bring themselves into line with international conventions on the subject, it being recognised now that private sector corruption can be equally harmful to the wellbeing of a country.

The distinction between public and non-public sector bribery is usually that it is unnecessary to prove that the public official's employer, the state, did not approve that the official should accept a benefit over and above his official salary. That goes without saying because it is a necessary implication from the way the law is stated,[1] whereas in the private sector lawful commission is a normal part of an employee's earnings. The private sector offence therefore requires proof that the employer or principal did not approve acceptance of the additional material benefit.

Whether concerned with the public or private sector, bribery

1 It is however quite possible that the defendant should raise as a defence the approval of his employer, the state, to his giving or receiving the bribe. If he adduces evidence to that effect, it would be for the prosecution to prove the contrary.

laws normally sanction the conduct of both the giver and the receiver. Both are usually liable to the same penalty, although the circumstances in each case may warrant a court passing a less severe sanction, or even no sanction, on one of the parties.

If bribery is at the heart of corruption, it must be said that the offence is often difficult to prove, especially the connection between the material benefit, sought, offered, given or accepted, and the exercise or non-exercise of the authorised function. In the case of public officials two other offences acknowledge the difficulty of proving bribery. One is a simple gift offence, less serious than bribery. The other is the offence of illicit enrichment or unexplained wealth.

Gift offence Some countries make it an offence for a public official to ask for or receive a material benefit for which he has not been given official permission. In most countries, only the public official is liable; in others the offeror or giver is also liable. Unlike the offence of bribery, there is no need to prove that the gift was given in connection with the performance or non-performance of the official's duties.

In public services where demanding or expecting gifts has become widespread, defining it as an offence has been shown to bring about a rapid reversal of this pernicious habit.

Illicit enrichment The offence of illicit enrichment reflects the public's feeling that an official whose wealth or life style is wholly out of keeping with his official salary owes the community an explanation. Unless he gives the court a satisfactory explanation of his wealth, he is guilty of the offence of illicit enrichment (or 'unexplained wealth' as it is sometimes called). Some countries have this offence, others do not, the latter taking the view that it is against a fundamental principle of their criminal justice system for a defendant to have to explain anything. Yet it is an offence found in the 1996 Inter-American Convention Against Corruption, the African Union Convention on Preventing and Combating Corruption and the recent UN Convention Against Corruption.

Abuse of authority or misuse of position As its name suggests, the offence of abuse of authority is committed by a person entrusted with a degree of authority who uses that authority to benefit himself. He takes advantage of his position in a way that is disapproved of by the community. The key idea underlying the offence is a breach of trust. The differences from bribery (which also involves a breach of trust) are that the breach does not necessarily involve a complicitous party and that the entrusted authority is not necessarily traded. The offence is not precisely defined and, for that reason, can apply to a wide range of conduct. It is usually applied to public officials[2] but in some countries the offence can apply to anyone entrusted with authority.

Trading in influence The offence of trading in influence is included in the UN Convention Against Corruption as a measure states should consider adding to their criminal law.[3] A number of civil law countries already have the offence. It can be described as bribery at one remove. The influence peddler solicits or accepts or agrees to accept an advantage in exchange for exerting improper influence on a public authority or for exerting influence on a public authority in order to obtain an undue benefit. It can be difficult to distinguish the offence from lawful lobbying. The essential difference is that either the influence brought to bear is unlawful or the granting of the benefit by the public authority is unlawful. In framing the offence great care is needed not to outlaw the lawful advocacy of any cause.

Other offences The offence of embezzlement is sometimes found in a country's anticorruption armoury and is mentioned in articles 17 and 22 of the UN Convention Against Corruption. The offence consists in the misappropriation by an employee or agent of his employer's or principal's property. It has little in common with bribery except that it involves a breach of trust in the same sense as any criminal act by an

2 As is recommended in article 19 of the UN Convention Against Corruption.
3 See article 18 UNCAC.

employee or agent in the course of his engagement. Although the offence is present in the penal code of every country, it is not usually found among the corruption offences and consequently is not usually included in the mandate of a specialised anticorruption agency.

In a few countries what is loosely described as 'economic and financial crime' has been included in the mandate of the anticorruption agency. Commercial fraud and theft fall into this category but it is obvious that, conceptually, fraud and theft have little in common with bribery. The reason why the investigation of economic and financial crime is given to a separate agency is usually because the police are seen as lacking the necessary expertise or are no longer trusted. But the inclusion of economic and financial crime in the mandate of an anticorruption body confuses the distinction between corruption and other criminality and undermines the rationale for a separate, specialised body to deal with corruption.

Money laundering, which is now made an offence in many countries, is another of those offences requiring some financial investigative skills. The money being laundered is usually the proceeds of crime but obviously the crime involved need not be a corruption offence. For that reason the investigation of money laundering is not usually made the exclusive preserve of the specialised anticorruption body.

Corruption-related crime Bribery is often used to facilitate other forms of criminality, especially serious and organised crime. A commercial fraud, for example, is often brought about by bribery. A drug dealer operates without hindrance from the authorities because the police are accepting payments from him. It is therefore essential that the mandate to investigate corruption should include the investigation of criminality suspected of being related to or facilitated by corruption in order to uncover the suspected underlying corruption.

Bribery of judges, arbitrators and sports officials Bearing in mind that corruption is the unauthorised trading of entrusted authority, there is no conceptual difficulty in condemning a judge, arbitrator, umpire or referee for accepting an inducement or reward intended to affect his decision. He may not be in the position of employee or agent owing a duty to an employer or principal but he is unarguably selling the authority he has been entrusted with, whether by the state, the parties to a dispute or the governing body of a sport. The community regards bent judges with contempt and the law against corruption should not hesitate to reflect that view. Those who are prepared to accept personal advantage for compromising the impartiality of the decision-making they have been entrusted with should be liable to sanction under the anticorruption law.

Bribery or treating of voters or candidates When it comes to bribing or treating voters at an election, the description 'unauthorised trading of entrusted authority' is more difficult to apply. A voter is not normally regarded as possessing entrusted authority; he is neither authorised to vote nor entrusted by anyone with a duty to vote. Except in those countries where voting in a parliamentary election is mandatory, he is free to choose whether or not to vote. He is also free to vote for any of the candidates. Yet in all modern states the law forbids a person from offering or giving a voter a personal advantage in exchange for his vote. The community expects the voter to exercise his right to vote unaffected by such inducement or reward and the law condemns anyone who seeks to affect the voter by that means. Whatever may be its conceptual foundation, the payment or 'treating' of voters is rightly regarded as an offence akin to the usual form of bribery and should therefore fall within the remit of the anticorruption body.

PERIPHERAL VALUES IN ADMINISTRATIVE LAW

If bribery can be regarded as the worm undermining a person's entrusted authority, its close relative is the undue advantage that can accrue from the conflict between a person's entrusted authority and his personal gain. In some countries profiting from, or even failing to declare, a conflict of interests is a criminal offence. In most countries the failure to declare a conflict of interests is a breach of a code of conduct, resulting in disciplinary or administrative sanction.[4]

Related to conflict of interests is the use of one's official position, actual or recently vacated, to obtain other engagement or employment in the private sector.[5] Codes of conduct therefore seek to restrict such soliciting and, for a certain time, any engagement or employment by parties with whom the public servant had official dealings.

THE USE OF CIVIL PROCEEDINGS

The civil law of modern states recognises that an act of corruption can form the basis for legal proceedings resulting in civil remedies. A contract obtained by bribery can be set aside; the parties who have failed to obtain the contract owing to the bribery paid by the party to whom the contract was awarded may be entitled to damages for their loss; the bribe itself and the assets acquired by the bribery can be recovered; those who have assisted in the transfer or disposal of the proceeds of corruption can be held liable in damages. These civil law remedies provide an increasingly effective means of ensuring that corruption does not pay and are usually to be found in the civil laws of modern states.

FINDING OUT, PROVING AND RECOVERING – INVESTIGATIVE, EVIDENTIAL AND ASSET RECOVERY PROVISIONS

It is obvious that a community value set out in the criminal law is there to be upheld. There would be no point in including corruption offences in the criminal law unless those offences could be effectively investigated, prosecuted and sanctioned.

4 Even in those countries where conflict of interests is not a criminal offence, the profiting from such a conflict would almost certainly amount to the offence of abuse of authority or misuse of position mentioned earlier.

5 This activity is sometimes known by the French term 'pantouflage'.

Corruption offences, however, are not easy to investigate and prove. It is therefore necessary that effective investigative and evidential provisions should be in place so that the corrupt can be justly dealt with. That justice should include the means of depriving them of their corrupt gains.

For the purpose of investigating alleged corruption offences the normal powers given to the police to enable them to investigate any criminality should also be given to the anticorruption authority. In addition to the usual powers of arrest, detention, search and seizure, the anticorruption authority should also have the power to intercept communications, to require suspects to attend and be questioned and to search for and examine bank accounts. It should also be able to apply for the retention of travel documents during investigation.

Evidential provisions should enable a court to infer conclusions of beneficial ownership of property and of corruption upon proof of certain facts. The court should be required to protect from disclosure in court the identity of any informant who is not called as a witness. The law should provide that a party to a corrupt transaction is not to be treated as an accomplice for the purpose of any law of evidence requiring the evidence of an accomplice to be corroborated.

As regards the recovery of the proceeds of corruption, the criminal court should have the power to order the forfeiture of any property it is satisfied was the result of the corrupt activity, whether or not a conviction resulted from the proceedings. Furthermore the legislature should consider allowing a court, on application by the prosecutor, to order forfeiture of any property seized during the investigation in respect of which nobody has made a justified claim within a certain period of the application.

Corruption offences can often be prosecuted successfully only if one party to the corrupt transaction is prepared to give evidence for the state against the other party. Whatever the general criminal procedure law may say, the anticorruption law should make clear that the public prosecutor may decide not to prosecute one party provided he gives true evidence against the other. Likewise, the court should be able to sanction a lesser sentence on a party who gives true evidence for the prosecution.

SANCTIONS

Bribery and related offences are regarded in most countries as serious crimes. That is reflected in a maximum penalty of imprisonment (usually of seven or even ten years) and/or unlimited fine to deal with the most serious case. Of course, most cases are relatively minor and do not merit anything like the maximum penalty. The sentencing court needs to have a sentencing discretion that allows it to impose an appropriate penalty. The law should therefore not specify minimum sentences: they fail to cater for the very minor offence and tend to be counterproductive in that courts become reluctant to convict if the only sentence that can follow is a minimum term of imprisonment.

In some countries removal from public office is a consequence of conviction for certain corruption offences. Suspension, for a certain period, of eligibility to stand for election, or be appointed, to public office can be made an automatic consequence of conviction. A court should also be able to prohibit the convicted person from taking or continuing employment for a certain period in any directing, managerial or professional capacity.

KEEPING IT SIMPLE

Policymakers and legislators are prone to make the law more all-embracing, more complicated and thus less intelligible than it need be. The values that the law against corruption seeks to uphold are simple and widely understood. It is incumbent on our leaders to ensure that the law is kept as simple and as clear as it can be, so that citizens can readily understand what the law says about the standards that they aspire to live by.[6]

Keeping it simple is, however, often more easily said than done. Here are a few practical suggestions:

6 The American expression 'bright line law' is intended to convey the idea of simplicity and clarity.

Ensure that the offences that are to be enforced by the anticorruption authority are kept to a minimum.
Exclude from the mandate of that authority any offence not connected to bribery. Embezzlement, fraud and 'economic crime' are examples of crimes that should be excluded unless they have been facilitated by bribery.
Ensure that reprehensible conduct that does not amount to one of the core bribery offences or some other criminality is dealt with by disciplinary measures taken by the employer or professional body.
Take particular care over the preparation of the law. Clarity and certainty cannot always result in brevity.
Policymakers and legislators should not let themselves be deflected by over-cautious opinions of legal advisers.
Be prepared to amend the law in the light of experience.

In conclusion, let us keep in mind that the laws against corruption are concerned with upholding certain values and that the object of a national policy against corruption is the upholding of those values. The effective and special way of upholding those values is the justification for dealing with corruption differently from other forms of criminality.

5
A National Strategy

INTRODUCTION

At the heart of corruption is bribery. That serious criminal offence reflects a community value contained in the criminal law of all modern states. It is, however, a difficult value to uphold by enforcement of the criminal law alone because the offence is committed secretly and complicitously by two people who are content, more or less, with their bargain. The result is that the offence is unlikely ever to come to light unless information is given to the authorities by a third person who knows or suspects that something unlawful has occurred. In addition, the world has learned from experience that enforcement is not enough. We have come to realise that tackling the widespread menace of corruption effectively requires more than enforcement. It requires a strategy, a strategy that contains two other elements: prevention and public education and support. The design of that strategy is the subject of this chapter.

A NATIONAL STRATEGY

Where corruption in a country has become widespread and deep-rooted, it has proved useless simply to enact stricter laws and harsher penalties. For much of the twentieth century that was the orthodox response of the authorities to a growing menace. It failed and the problem got worse. The world came to recognise that a national struggle against corruption required a strategy that would apply to the whole country and, without exception, to all sectors of the community. A problem that had spread throughout the public service inevitably would also have spread to the private sector and every other part of the community. Treating corruption only in the public sector, as has been the case in most countries and continues to the case in some, is like trying to treat a disease of the blood only in the arteries but not in the veins.

Once the government has taken the political decision that corruption is to be fought and overcome, it will need to articulate and adopt a strategy against corruption. The overall objective of the strategy is to reduce corruption to the point where it no longer undermines the development of the country.

Much confusion has arisen about what is meant by a strategy against corruption. Many countries have been persuaded to adopt what is called a National Anticorruption Strategy but is not a strategy at all. The so-called strategy is no more than a long list of activities, most of which are intended to improve governance. It is worth repeating that governance, which is about how things are run, is not the same as anticorruption, which is concerned with upholding certain values. The conflating of these two distinct notions and the resulting confusion are the principal cause of the worldwide lack of progress in the fight against corruption. A strategy is the plan by which an objective is to be achieved; it is not a list of activities but is the means by which activities are to be carried out to achieve the objective.

The strategy for fighting corruption is simple, comprehensive, clear and coherent. It consists of three elements: first, enforcement of the laws against corruption by investigating, prosecuting, trying and punishing breaches of those laws; second, prevention of corruption by minimising in systems and procedures the opportunities for corrupt activity; third, the education of the community about corruption and the development of public support for the fight.

The strategy is comprehensive in that the laws against corruption apply to everyone and every sector; it is not limited to the public sector. It is comprehensive also in the sense that it engages every part of the community to become actively involved in the fight, and in the sense that all the systems and procedures by which society organises its affairs are liable to anticorruption scrutiny.

Each element of the strategy has its own clear objective. Enforcement punishes corrupt conduct, prevention seeks to eliminate opportunities for corruption from the systems and procedures by which we regulate our affairs, and education and public support first gets people to join the fight and secondly seeks to bring about a change of attitude to corruption in every individual of the community. The coherence of the strategy arises from the necessity that these three elements should be applied together in coordination. They support each other and are interdependent: any success in one element enhances the other two. Experience has shown that none of them on its own can deal with corruption effectively. The key to success lies in the coordinated implementation of all three elements, together and at the same time.

The coherence of the strategy also derives from the clarity of its overall objective (the control of corruption), its purpose distinguished from the purpose of governance (the upholding of a set of values as opposed to the way of running things), and the coordination and interdependence of its three elements.

THE ELEMENTS OF THE STRATEGY

It is necessary now to say a little more about each of the elements of the strategy before turning to their coordination and interdependence.

Enforcing the law against corruption begins with investigation. In most countries investigation is carried out with a view to prosecution, but in reality only a small proportion of investigations will culminate in prosecution. Corruption can be difficult to investigate – the evidence is often hard to find and secure. More often than not the prosecutor will advise that the prospects of a successful prosecution are weak and do not justify proceeding to trial. The investigation may however have revealed that a disciplinary or administrative breach of a code of conduct may have been committed. In that event the matter is referred to the suspect's employer or professional body so that it can decide whether to take disciplinary measures.

In almost all forms of criminality, investigation starts with information provided by the victim of the crime or a witness to it. Investigating corruption has the difficulty that the corrupt transaction is not usually witnessed by a third party nor do either of the parties to the transaction regard themselves as victims ready to report the matter. This difficulty is compounded by the ambivalent attitude to corruption that people have who live in a country where the problem has long been a fact of daily life. The result is that information about corrupt activity is hard to come by. It is why the orthodox reaction of the authorities to a growing problem – harsher laws, heavier penalties – has no effect. Unless people can be persuaded to voice their suspicions to the authorities, corruption investigators are powerless.

The point of the public education and support element of the strategy now becomes clear. People need to understand why corruption is a bad thing; it is not a self-evident proposition. Then they need to understand how they can individually play their part in the fight against it. A crucial part is to come forward to the authorities and report what they believe to be happening. But there are many causes that make people unwilling to do that. Ambivalence, indifference, apathy, tolerance, resignation and fear have to be addressed if information is to start flowing. This immediate objective of the public education and support element of the strategy is given further consideration later in this chapter, as is the more important, long-term objective of bringing about a complete change in people's attitude to corruption. For the moment it is the close link between the enforcement and public education elements of the strategy that deserves emphasis.

The prevention element concerns itself with the systems and procedures by which a community orders its affairs. Each of us is involved with several of these systems and procedures every day, whether at work or elsewhere. These hundreds of processes – whether for the granting of a large defence contract, or the purchase of supplies for a factory, or the obtaining of a driving licence, or the award of a school place at the village school, or medical care at the local clinic – can all present an opportunity for corruption. It is wrong to expose those who work in or use these systems to the daily temptation of taking corrupt advantage of the system. It is an essential function of good management to ensure that such opportunities are eliminated so far as possible.

It is this element of the strategy that most closely resembles governance. There is an obvious overlap in the measures needed to eliminate the opportunity for corruption and those needed to ensure that things are properly and efficiently run. But the objectives of anticorruption and good governance are not the same and it is necessary to keep the difference clearly in mind, even when it is difficult in practice to see the distinction between the two.

It is self-evident that the measures put in place to prevent corruption reinforce the message of public education that corrupt conduct is wrong. Likewise, an understanding of corruption and the harm it does encourages those who work in systems and processes to devise and apply effective preventive measures in those systems and processes. These two elements of the strategy reinforce each other. Knowing where the opportunities for corruption exist allows the educational message to be relevantly and accurately targeted. The more effective the preventive measures, the fewer the instances of corrupt conduct. The greater the disapproval of corrupt conduct, the more information provided to the anticorruption authorities. The more effective the enforcement, the greater the deterrence and the greater the willingness to provide information. This interdependence makes the three elements equally important, a point that is often overlooked and that those most closely involved in the fight have constantly to be reminded of.

The combined result of the three elements creates a momentum in society. Growing public support has a snowball effect.

Before long people see that things can change, that they themselves can change. The prospect of a transformation begins to appear realistic. However, for this to happen the three elements have to work together in close coordination. The coordinated implementation of the elements of the strategy is the fourth essential for success and will be the subject of the next chapter.

At this stage it is worth exploring some of the implications of adopting an anticorruption strategy that applies to the whole country and to every part of the community. Reference was made in chapter 2 to the policy of investigating every corruption allegation capable of investigation and the reasons underlying that policy. The policy is so fundamental to the success of the fight against corruption that the reasons for its adoption should be repeated:

1. What appears to be a minor matter quite often unravels into a much more serious case.
2. For the citizen who has brought himself to make a complaint, the matter will be important. If it is dismissed as unimportant, he is unlikely ever to return to the authorities, perhaps with a crucial piece of information. If community support is to be won, the minor complaint must be taken seriously.
3. Picking and choosing which reports to investigate and which to ignore gives rise to suspicion of improper influence having affected the decision or, worse, of corruption in the investigating unit.
4. Ignoring some complaints gives the impression that some corruption is tolerated, that double standards apply.
5. The fact is that widespread small-scale corruption does serious damage to the wellbeing of a country. Furthermore, a single small act of corruption can have catastrophic consequences; instances come readily to mind in the field of security or public health.

These are the reasons why the natural tendency to focus on only the most important matters must be resisted. Linked to this tendency is the desire to initiate investigative action against a particular suspect without waiting for a report of corruption to be made against him. Targeting suspects in this way is a recipe for failure. Before long the public will be led to believe that the targeting is being done for political reasons. When that happens, people lose confidence in the impartiality of investigation. A recent trend has developed of identifying the sectors of the economy most vulnerable to corrupt exploitation and to encourage the anticorruption authorities to focus their activities on those sectors. While it would be correct to give priority to those sectors with regard to prevention and education, it would be wrong for the reason already mentioned to target them for investigative action without first receiving a report of a corrupt transaction.

A strategy applying to the whole country and an investigation policy that requires a response to reports received even from far-flung parts of the country requires the anticorruption authorities to have a presence that covers the whole country. It is not enough for the authorities to confine themselves to the commercial and financial centres. They must have outposts farther afield, in the outlying communities. That reality has resource and organisational implications that will be explored in subsequent chapters.

6
The Strategy in Action

INTRODUCTION

At the end of the previous chapter, the need to coordinate the implementation of the three elements of the national strategy against corruption was explained. The implications of an investigation policy that requires every pursuable allegation of corruption to be investigated and the necessity for the anticorruption authorities to be present not only in the commercial and financial centre but also in the outlying communities were touched on. This chapter begins with the coordinated implementation of the three elements of the strategy before considering the main features of an anticorruption body and its accountability and independence.

THE COORDINATED IMPLEMENTATION OF THE STRATEGY

How can the coordinated implementation of the strategy best be achieved? A couple of examples of the sort of operational coordination needed may serve to point the way to the solution that many countries have now adopted.

Let us imagine that a senior inspector of taxes has been arrested, tried and convicted for accepting large bribes from taxpayers in return for minimising their tax liability. He was behaving in this way for several years under the noses of the senior management of the tax department. The system the inspector was required to work in provided him the opportunity to take advantage of it. After the imprisonment of one of his senior inspectors the head of the department is ready to accept a suggestion that corruption prevention specialists and his staff should together examine the system in order to eliminate any corruption opportunities. Let us also consider the frame of mind of the staff of the department. They are probably in a state of shock; the inspector, their longstanding and well-liked colleague, is now serving a long stretch. This is the time to talk to them about corruption and their part in fighting it.

The second example: let us suppose that anticorruption investigators are engaged in a covert investigation in the procurement department of the defence ministry. The covert operation has gone on for some time and has reached a critical stage. The last thing needed at this point is for the corruption prevention specialists or the educators to come tramping in over the territory. It is essential that the investigators should know what the other two groups are planning.

Clearly this kind of close coordination and mutual reinforcement is easier to manage under one roof than by three separate agencies of government. Indeed, there has not yet been a successful example of the three elements being put into effect by three separate, existing institutions of government. Apart from the obvious difficulty of getting three separate bodies to cooperate to the extent necessary for success, each of these bodies will have its own portfolio of responsibility; the grafting on of an anticorruption role is unlikely to be given the priority it should have. Nor is the staff of these bodies likely to have the expertise required. It is because tackling corruption requires special treatment, unlike other forms of criminality, that so many countries have decided that a separate, specialised agency is needed to lead the implementation of the three elements of the anticorruption strategy. In many countries an added impetus for the creation of a separate agency is the fact that the usual investigative authority, the police, has itself become so corrupt that it can no longer be trusted to investigate any criminality, let alone corruption.

THE BASIC FEATURES OF AN ANTICORRUPTION BODY

A word first to remind ourselves what an anticorruption body is supposed to do, and then a word about what it should not be required to do.

As an executive agency, its function is to lead the implementation of the national anticorruption strategy. It is required to advance all three elements of the strategy, simultaneously and in coordination with each other. It is there to give the community the lead in upholding the anticorruption values set out in the law in the form of the anticorruption offences clustered around the core offence of bribery.

If the anticorruption body is required to take the lead in the fight against corruption and is to be held accountable to the community, it should be sole leader. Leadership by two or more in this sort of struggle is rarely effective and shared responsibility is often a device of evasion, blurring the lines of accountability to the community. We all need to have a clear idea of who leads, who is responsible for receiving and acting on our information, and to whom we should turn for guidance.

The anticorruption body should not be required to deal with other criminality unless that other criminality is connected to or facilitated by corruption. Dealing with offences that have no connection to corruption undermines the raison d'être of an agency specially created to deal with a special sort of crime. Other criminality should be investigated by the police. The anticorruption body should not be regarded as an alternative police force.

Nor should the anticorruption body be regarded as the engine of governance reform, as currently often happens. In many countries governance reform is most necessary but that should be the job of the administration, not the anticorruption body.

Finally, the anticorruption body should not be the prosecutor of corruption offences. It is an important safeguard against oppressive prosecution that investigation and prosecution should be the responsibility of separate organs. The long-standing separation of investigation, prosecution and trial should be maintained.

It should therefore be unnecessary to add that the anticorruption body should not itself decide guilt or innocence or impose sanctions. It should be able to summon and question suspects and witnesses but should not be empowered to hold hearings, whether public or not. It is necessary to say it only because this option has been tried, with disastrous results.

Given that corruption is a national problem and that coercive powers are needed for its effective investigation, it is inevitable that an anticorruption body with the responsibility of leading the national anticorruption strategy should be an agency of the state, funded by the public purse. In view of the duties and responsibilities it is to be given, the anticorruption body should be established by primary law, not by executive decision.

The law sets out the status and title of the body, its functions and powers, its method of funding and accountability, and the appointment and tenure of its head. It is important that the head be responsible for the appointment and conduct of its staff. Since the body is to have strong investigative powers, it should be a disciplined service with clear lines of authority and responsibility, culminating in the head. The head should therefore be the appointing and disciplinary authority for the staff, including the power of dismissal when the integrity of an officer is in doubt. The organisation cannot put the campaign against corruption at risk by continuing to employ any officer of questionable integrity.

The mandate of the anticorruption body should be clearly and succinctly stated in the law. Its functions are to investigate with a view to prosecution all allegations of corruption capable of investigation, to provide corruption prevention advice to the public service and to the private sector, and to educate the public about corruption and enlist its support. The mandate states the national strategy, the implementation of which the anticorruption body is intended to lead.

The organisational structure of the anticorruption body will almost certainly have to reflect its three-part mandate and its character as a disciplined service. The latter demands a hierarchical structure led by its head. The three parts of the mandate entail three different kinds of work carried out by officers with different sets of skills. It is natural therefore that these different sets of officers should be organised into three operational departments – investigation, prevention and public education and support. At the core of this structure is an administration department dealing with finances, personnel and supplies. So there it is – a three-sided pyramid with an administrative core.

It is here that a most important feature of an effective anti-corruption body should be identified. One of the seven essentials of success set out in chapter 2 is public support. Without strong public support the anticorruption drive will fail. Passive approval is insufficient. What is required is the active support and involvement of the community. What has proved to be one of the most active forms of support and involvement of the community is the use by the anticorruption body of advisory committees of citizens in the three elements of its work. More will be said about these committees in chapter 8. For the moment it is enough to say that the law should simply provide that advisory committees may be appointed to assist the anti-corruption body in the performance of its duties.

ACCOUNTABILITY

The law will state that the body is to be funded from public monies, that its accounts are to be audited by the state auditor and that it is to present an annual report of its activities to the executive or the legislature or both. More will be said about funding in chapter 7. It is self-evident that the body should keep proper accounts of its expenditure and have them audited. An annual report of its activities is a normal and important aspect of accountability but whether it should report to the executive or the legislature or both has been the subject of much discussion. As an agency of the administration, the body should report to the head of the executive, who should have to table the report in the legislature. It would be normal for a standing committee of the legislature to include the anticorruption body within its overview portfolio. Mention of these two lines of accountability is the moment to refer to the other three lines of accountability that an anticorruption body should have.

First, it is a consequence of the separation of investigation and prosecution that the conduct of investigators in carrying out their investigations will come under the scrutiny of the public prosecutor when the matter is referred to him for prosecution. Any misconduct by the investigators during the investigation may affect the decision to prosecute. Furthermore, the conduct of investigators will come under the scrutiny of the trial court and may affect the outcome of the trial. Investigators therefore carry out their investigations fully aware that they will be accountable for their conduct to the public prosecutor and to the court.

Second, the citizen advisory committees mentioned earlier provide perhaps the closest form of accountability. These committees are involved in the daily work of the three operational departments of the anticorruption body. In providing advice, they monitor closely the work of the body and they report separately and directly to the executive and the legislature.

Third, the anticorruption body accounts directly to the community through the media. If the trust and support of the community is to be won, the body's use of the media to communicate with the public is essential. Properly conducted relations with the press are a vital part of the anticorruption body's daily work.

These six lines of accountability – to the executive, the legislature, the public prosecutor, the courts, the advisory committees and the public directly through the media – ensure that the anticorruption body is fully answerable for its conduct.

INDEPENDENCE

Independence and operational autonomy are central features of an effective anticorruption body. Independence is always relative and it follows that the more effective the systems of accountability, the greater the degree of independence that can be given. As always, the degree of independence depends on practical details.

The law should provide for the appointment, tenure and removal of the head and his deputy. Many variations of these matters are found in countries that have anticorruption bodies. This chapter looks at the proven best practices. Given the level at which corruption will have to be dealt with in all three elements of the strategy, the head of the anticorruption body should be at ministerial or permanent secretary rank. To mark the importance of the post, the appointment should be made by the head of state from two candidates proposed by the prime minister after consultation with the leader of the opposition.

The position of head of an anticorruption body is demanding and nobody should be expected to do the job indefinitely. A limited fixed term is desirable. While it would be natural to want to retain indefinitely an incumbent who is perceived to be doing a good job, the wisdom of resisting that impulse has been demonstrated time and again in the worlds of public affairs and private enterprise. A fresh pair of eyes at the top every few years has proved salutary. A single term of four or five years seems appropriate.

The need for security of tenure for certain posts in the public service is recognised in many countries. The rationale is usually the necessity of decision-making free from any self-consideration of job security. The post of head of the anticorruption body should carry the security of tenure applicable to the post of the state prosecutor or the auditor-general. That security is usually provided by specifying removal only on grounds of incompetence and by following a special procedure.

Additionally, in doing the job the incumbent should not have an eye to his next post, especially in the public service. It is therefore preferable for the appointment as head of the anticorruption body to be the last before normal retirement. While it may be suggested that a final posting carries the risk of the appointee making a quiet life his first priority, the reality of the administrative service of all countries shows many instances of senior administrators effectively deploying their energy and experience, even after retirement.

In the case of an anticorruption body structured in three operational departments (prevention, education and investigation), comprising staff with very different skills and backgrounds, the job of the head consists largely in ensuring that the three departments pull together in the same direction. This requirement and the desirability of a fresh outlook periodically make it preferable for any subsequent appointment as head to be made not by promotion from within but by selection from outside the organisation.

The law should say specifically that, in discharging his responsibilities, the head of the anticorruption body is not to be subject to the control or direction of any person except the head of state. It should be noted that any direction that might be given would have to be lawful. And to be lawful the direction would have to be consistent with the anticorruption law. Where the law provides that the duty of the body is to investigate every pursuable allegation of corruption, it would be unlawful to direct the body not to investigate a particular matter. It would also be unlawful to direct the body to investigate a particular matter unless the body had received an allegation regarding that matter.

As regards the post of the deputy head, there is a need both to provide institutional continuity and to avoid creating an indefinite promotion blockage while at the same time ensuring that the head and the deputy head can work in close harmony. Appointment to the deputy post from within the anticorruption body would provide institutional continuity. Appointing for a limited term would ensure that the appointment would not create an unduly lengthy promotion blockage. Appointment for a fixed term, renewable only once, would allow any incompatibility between the incumbents of the posts of head and deputy head to be ended at the expiry of the first term. The appointment of deputy head should also be made by the head of state upon the nomination of a candidate by the prime minister after consultation with the leader of the opposition. It should consist of a fixed term of three years renewable once only.

The law should provide that the head may appoint, on such terms and conditions as he sees fit, such officers as he needs to enable him to carry out his functions. That does not give him carte blanche to appoint as many officers as he likes. Appointments can be made only to posts that have been created and funded in the normal way through government estimates approved by the legislature.

The question now arises: on what terms and conditions should officers be employed in the anticorruption body? Officers will be recruited both from the public service and the private sector. Investigators, for example, will have to come from what is normally the only source of trained investigators, the police, at least initially before the anticorruption body has developed its own training capacity.

Although the anticorruption body is an organ of the administration funded by public monies voted by the legislature and is therefore a part of the public service, it should not form part of the civil service nor be subject to the law governing the civil service, in particular the disciplinary rules and procedures applicable to civil servants. Civil service permanent and pensionable terms of service are not desirable for officers of an anticorruption body, for the simple reason that, once on the payroll, staff tend to stay for good and the turnover rate is minimal. Civil service disciplinary procedures are lengthy and cumbersome and rarely result in dismissal. Furthermore, if officers of the anticorruption body are civil servants dependent on the central administration for their salaries and prospects of advancement, they cannot but be affected in the way they carry out their job when confronting certain parts of the administration.

Employment on contract for fixed, renewable terms with an end-of-contract gratuity in lieu of pension has a number of advantages for both the employee and employer. First, the prospect of a lump sum after a relatively short time, say three years, for a large purchase such as a car or the deposit on a house or children's education has proved to be a real attraction for a civil servant in mid-career. Second, the renewability of the contract allows a career to be made in the anticorruption body. Third, the organisation can be kept clear of unsatisfactory employees by ample notice of non-renewal, an important consideration for the elite corps that the anticorruption body should become. Fourth, the setting-up of a discrete pension scheme becomes unnecessary. Finally, for a civil servant contemplating a spell of service in the anticorruption body, if the administration is able to ensure a return to the civil service, the prospect of moving to the anticorruption body becomes more attractive when he has the option to return in due course to the civil service. The option should be of limited duration, say the duration of two contracts, for it would be unreasonable to expect the administration to keep the post in reserve indefinitely.

Unlike the system of attachment or secondment, this system of renewable contracts allows the individual concerned to cease being a civil servant for the duration of the contract and to become wholly the responsibility of the head of the anticorruption body. On returning to the civil service the individual should be permitted to 'buy back' any years of pensionable service lost by the years of service with the anticorruption body.

The system of contract employment has proved its worth and attraction for the anticorruption body and for its officers, whether recruited from the civil service or the private sector. The concern that the fixed term contract might result in a rapid turnover of officers has proved unfounded: job satisfaction on the part of the officers and investment in experience and advanced training by management has ensured a mutually beneficial tendency to keep renewing the fixed term contract.

It will not have escaped notice that these remarks about terms and conditions of service have been made under the heading 'independence'. The arrangements under which an officer is expected to do a difficult job go to the heart of the anticorruption body's independence, operational autonomy and impartiality. Nor will it have escaped notice that nothing has been said about remuneration. This all-important aspect of employment is considered in the next chapter dealing with resources.

The independence of an anticorruption body depends also on the nature of its funding. The body should be beholden to no individual or institution for its funds. It is the reason why the body should rely on public monies voted by the legislature. That is not to say that the national effort against corruption cannot accept assistance, whether financial or in kind, from other sources. It can and normally does, provided that such assistance is appropriately approved before it is received.

Independence is also marked by the operational autonomy of the anticorruption body. In all three arms of its operations, decisions rest with the body itself. In doing its work, it should not have to rely on any other body. It should therefore be given powers of arrest, detention, search, seizure, interception and access, and should not have to rely on the police for the exercise of these powers in the course of operations.

THE STRATEGY IN ACTION

Returning to the title of this chapter, it is time to say a little about the daily work of an anticorruption body in leading the implementation of the national strategy. Recalling that the strategy comprises the three elements of enforcement, prevention and public education and support, let us consider briefly what is involved in carrying out each of them.

As regards enforcement, the anticorruption body is concerned only with the first part of the enforcement process, namely investigation. Prosecution and trial, or disciplinary proceedings, are the responsibility of others. Investigation begins with a report received by the anticorruption body alleging the commission of a corruption offence. For the reasons previously explained, the investigation department begins an investigation only when it receives a report; it does not begin an investigation of its own initiative.

As soon as a report is received and the senior management of the investigation department decides that the matter is capable of being investigated, an investigation file is opened and allocated to one of the investigation units. The investigation is conducted with a view to prosecution.

As already pointed out, in reality the great majority of investigations will not end in prosecution, simply because the evidence needed to secure a conviction cannot be found. The role of managing investigations includes the regular review of progress made so as to determine whether further investigation is warranted or not. If yes, the point will be reached where the investigators believe the evidence of guilt is sufficient and they will submit the file to the public prosecutor for his decision on prosecution. If not, or if the prosecutor decides not to prosecute, the file will be closed on the decision of the head of the anticorruption body. More accurately the file will be marked 'no further action' for prosecution, since the matter might be reopened if the missing evidence materialises.

The process of closure of a file requires that the recommendation of the investigator of 'no further action' be endorsed by his supervisors and senior management. Before the file reaches the head of the anticorruption body, it goes to the investigation review committee, an advisory committee of citizens referred to in chapter 2 and described more fully in chapter 8, for its advice on the investigating officer's recommendation.

While the evidence may have been insufficient for prosecution, the investigation may have revealed evidence of a breach of internal rules of conduct. The investigating officer's recommendation may therefore include a recommendation that the disciplinary aspects of the matter be referred to the suspect's employer for consideration of disciplinary action.

As regards the corruption prevention element of the strategy, the work of eliminating opportunities for corrupt conduct from systems and procedures has two aspects. The first is the examination of existing or proposed systems and procedures and making changes to them. The second is the preparation of guidance for guarding against corruption in certain systems and procedures that are commonly found in the various departments and ministries of any administration, such as procurement contracts or the control of sensitive information.

The provision of specialist advice by the anticorruption body's prevention department to ministries and departments and to the private sector has to proceed on the basis of client/adviser. That basis arises from two features of corruption prevention. First, there is no compulsion that can be applied to a recalcitrant client in the administration except political pressure applied by the head of the administration. Second, the client and the adviser together have to examine the offending system and together have to devise the solution that eliminates the corruption opportunity if the proposed solution is to be applied successfully by those who operate the system.

The work of corruption prevention can and should be programmed. The department's annual work plan lists the systems and procedures to be examined during the year. The list and the order of priority are informed by the reports of corruption received from the public and the advice of the prevention advisory committee. The committee will also advise on the recommendations proposed for the system under review before the report is endorsed by the head of the anticorruption body and issued to the client department or ministry. A copy of the report is sometimes sent to the office of the head of the administration, whose responsibility for the public service extends to ensuring that corruption prevention measures are implemented in its ministries and departments.

As regards the public education and support element of the strategy, let us first consider what educating the whole community entails. There are two objectives: one that must be reached quickly, the other that can be achieved only in the long term. First, investigating corruption needs information from those who know what is going on. But people are usually most reluctant to provide information to the authorities. They must quickly be encouraged to do so in order that the enforcement side of the strategy can show the results that the community wants to see. The long-term objective is nothing less than bringing about a change of attitude to corruption in everyone in the community, an objective that many have dismissed as impossible but that has been shown in a few places to be entirely feasible.

We should realise that educating the whole community means every sector and every age group, every rank from the highest to the most humble. Our leaders – politicians, senior officials and judges – need to understand as much as do schoolchildren and students why corruption is a bad thing (not a self-evident proposition) and what each of them can do to help fight the problem.

As in any other sphere, the means of getting the messages across are broadly two: face-to-face communication (meetings, talks, seminars, training, etc) and mass communication (radio, television, print media, posters, internet, etc).

It is clear that the task of educating the whole community is much too large for the anticorruption body alone. It will never have the means to recruit enough educators and communicators. It must therefore make use of the community's own teachers and leaders.

Like the work of prevention, the work of education and public support can be programmed. An obvious division of labour separates the mass communication work from the face-to-face work. Two divisions of specialists planning their work for the year ahead in consultation with the other two operational departments, investigation and prevention, produces the coordinated approach essential to success. The face-to-face division will target its audiences, whether senior officials, judges, police recruits, business managers, schoolchildren or business school graduates. The message to be conveyed will be tailored accordingly. The mass communication division will divide its budget between the different means of communication, and its messages will convey particular themes. There is no limit to the creativity of educators and communicators in getting the anticorruption message across, especially with the help of their advisory committee.

7
Resources

INTRODUCTION

It is perhaps stating the obvious that tackling a phenomenon that is undermining every aspect of a country's development and has spread to every sector of the community will require substantial resources if the effort is to succeed. In reality it may not be that obvious. Looking at the countries that have decided to tackle corruption by enacting laws and creating an anticorruption body manned by a handful of officers, the most common cause of failure is the lack of resources put into the fight. On the assumption that our leaders have the will to address the problem, it seems that time and again they fail to consider the quantity of resources needed and the financial costs involved. This chapter identifies the relevant factors and indicates an answer to the minister of finance's question: how much will all this cost?

THE COST CENTRE

Since the financial cost of fighting corruption lies largely in the salaries of the officers directly engaged in the task, it is not difficult to work out the wages bill. If the officers are grouped together in one body, the costs of common administration, equipment, accommodation, services and supplies are easily arrived at. An incidental advantage of a single anticorruption body is that the cost centre is more readily identified and quantified.

PUBLIC FUNDS FOR A NATIONAL PROBLEM

There can be little doubt that a state agency required to lead the implementation of a national strategy against a national problem ought to be funded by public monies voted by the legislature. Its estimates therefore form part of the government's annual estimates.

The process of preparing those estimates is an annual ritual of negotiating with the ministry of finance for a slice of the resource pie, in competition with the big-spending departments like health and education. The setting of spending priorities is the job of the government and it is for the government to decide what priority to give to the fight against corruption: just how important is it for the country to overcome corruption?

NATIONAL FACTORS

The number of officers needed depends on a number of factors: the size of the population, the size of the public service and the size of the police force and other disciplined services. The geographical size of the country must be taken into account since far-flung branches must be self-sufficient in manpower and cannot usually rely on operational assistance from the centre. The investigative element of the strategy requires substantially more manpower than the other two and a policy of investigating all allegations capable of investigation means that the manpower must be sufficient to respond promptly to allegations received.

THE COMPONENTS OF EXPENDITURE

As mentioned above, by far the largest item of an anticorruption body's budget is the salaries of officers. As public servants, there is a case for paying them higher salaries than civil servants only if the salaries of the latter have fallen so low that they no longer provide a decent standard of living. If people of quality are to be recruited and retained, the salaries paid in the private sector for equivalent jobs provide a useful guide. It must be recognised that officers of the anticorruption body are unlikely to be allowed to supplement their salaries by secondary employment, an option that may be available to other public servants.

Experience suggests that salaries and other emoluments account for about 90% of an anticorruption body's recurrent expenditure. The remainder of recurrent expenditure covers office and special equipment, vehicle maintenance, accommodation costs (rent or maintenance), services, supplies and operational and project costs.

EXPERIENCE ELSEWHERE

What then of the finance minister's question: how much? For the purpose of this chapter, it is unnecessary to attempt to arrive at a figure in dollars or euros or any other currency. Indeed, such a figure would signify little since salaries vary greatly from country to country.

What can be done, however, is to indicate to the minister and his cabinet colleagues that experience elsewhere indicates that a country intent on succeeding against corruption should spend annually on the fight up to 0.5% of its national recurrent budget.

A couple of points that may provide a little comfort to the minister: the full amount of money will not be needed from year one; it will take four or five years for the anticorruption body to build up to its full capacity. Secondly, the posts required for the body need not all be new: some could be redeployed from other parts of the administration. Thirdly, as the anticorruption campaign takes effect and the economy grows, that figure of 0.5% is likely to drop gradually each year.

THE GOVERNMENT'S COMMITMENT

If there is a determination, usually from a government that is newly elected, to combat corruption, it is essential, as indicated in the earlier chapter on political will, that the cabinet, in giving policy approval, should also be aware of the approximate amount of financial resources that will be needed and express its commitment in principle to providing those resources.

Thereafter the community should keep a close eye on the government's annual estimates, in particular on the proportion that the anticorruption estimate bears to the whole. It should rise steadily as the anticorruption campaign builds. Any decline in that proportion in the first few years is a sure sign of weakening political will.

OTHER SOURCES

In many of the countries that most need to confront corruption, the public treasury has become so impoverished that the financial burden of undertaking or maintaining the fight against corruption is believed to be impossible without other sources of funding. That belief is reinforced by the willingness of donors to help. The dangers arising from that willingness are of two kinds.

The first arises from the good intentions of the international donor community and is perhaps the more difficult to guard against. Donations, whether loans or grants, from multilateral and bilateral donors come with 'conditionalities' attached. Conditionality usually means that aid will continue only if the recipient country goes about dealing with corruption in the way suggested by the donor or achieves targets and results, both often unrealistic, at least in the area of anticorruption.

In consequence, countries that want to deal with corruption and accept outside financial help to do so often find that they no longer control the agenda. Not only is the risk of an aid-dependent mentality increased but the unrealistic targets and results expectation makes this source of funding unreliable – these funds can dry up from one year to the next. To cap it all, to the extent that international aid reduces the amount that the taxpayer invests in the fight against corruption, so is the commitment of the community to the fight undermined.

Increasingly, international and bilateral donors insist on carrying out a 'governance assessment' in order to 'determine the priorities, modalities and volume of aid'.[1] One result is that the beneficiary country is likely to have even less say on how it

1 See 'Donor Approaches to Governance Assessment' from the Network on Governance of the OECD's Development Assistance Committee, January 2009.

deals with corruption. Another consequence is that the worse the assessment, the less aid a country is likely to receive – a curious way of preventing a state from failing.

The second kind of danger arising from funding that is not public money is the compromising of the anticorruption effort itself. Donations, in cash or in kind, from business interests, for example, may not be made purely in the public interest. An allegation of corruption concerning a large benefactor of the anticorruption body may not receive the impartial consideration that it should. A public perception that the anticorruption body's impartiality has been bought will destroy public trust and support.

These dangers do not mean that an anticorruption body should never accept outside financial help. What is needed is an independent decision on whether an offer of assistance, in cash or in kind, can properly be accepted. The government should establish a small committee to advise on the matter. Clearly, an offer of assistance from the World Bank will be regarded in a quite different light from an offer from a large local enterprise. The law should provide for the establishment of such a committee to advise on the acceptance of outside assistance to the anticorruption body.

8
Community Support

INTRODUCTION

It is now generally recognised that an anticorruption body on its own, or even the government on its own, cannot succeed in defeating corruption. A widespread problem that has affected the whole community requires public support if it is to be overcome.

By 'public support' is meant the active participation of the community, not merely the expression of support for the cause from the sidelines. But active public support is hard to come by. People do not see why they should become actively involved when it is the anticorruption body that has been given the job. Surely the community can breathe a sigh of relief that it is not their job and need only approve of the efforts of the anticorruption body.

That view is profoundly mistaken. Unless the community's active support is developed, the anticorruption body alone cannot beat corruption. It is worth repeating that the support of the community is one of the essentials of success against corruption. Without it, any anticorruption strategy fails. If the anticorruption strategy can be regarded as the spear of the nation against corruption, the anticorruption body as the spearhead can achieve little without the shaft of public engagement. The anticorruption body must engage the public service institutions, the private sector enterprises and the community-based organisations in active participation.

When an anticorruption body has been created, there is a real risk that the departments, agencies and ministries of the administration itself will sit back. They will leave it to the anticorruption body without providing their active help. The public sector is a major part of the problem of corruption. It is incumbent on the management of the entities of the public sector to ensure that each of those entities plays its role in being part of the solution.

A number of measures are needed to ensure that active public support is developed. They should be taken by the anticorruption body itself and by the national administration, the legislature, the judiciary, the business sector and all the other sectors of the community. This chapter considers the measures that should be taken by each of these participants. First, however, it describes the general approach to bringing the community on side.

ENGAGING THE COMMUNITY AT THE OUTSET

In chapter 3 the ways of strengthening the political will to tackle corruption were discussed. One of them was the government's consultation of the opinion-formers of the community, the purpose of which is, first, to inform the community of the main issues that arise in fighting corruption and of the government's initial thinking and, second, to seek the views of the opinion-formers on these issues. The consultation should be done before the government decides how to implement a national strategy against corruption and should involve opinion-formers in all sectors and at all levels. The fact that the government takes the trouble to consult the community at once gives people the encouragement to express their views, views that will be taken into account in formulating the implementation plan. The issues themselves indicate how they will directly affect the community.

USING THE TEACHERS

Once the anticorruption body is operational, its education department will seek to reach the community broadly in two ways: mass communication and direct face-to-face communication. The intention here is not to explore the details of the methods of the education department's work, but rather to repeat the point that the department itself will never have enough educators and communicators to carry the anticorruption message to every part of the community. In direct communication it must rely on the leaders of the community to convey the message to their employees, members, trainees, students, audiences and congregations. It is therefore crucially important that the anticorruption body enlist the support of the community's leaders from the outset, for they are the ones who can most effectively get the message across. They will not be persuaded overnight to come on board; it takes time. But it must be done.

ESTABLISHING ADVISORY COMMITTEES

The anticorruption body must win and retain the trust and confidence of the public if it is to succeed. One of the best ways of doing that is to let people see that it is doing its job honestly, competently and fearlessly, and is not abusing its powers. Furthermore the advice of citizens experienced in various walks of life provides invaluable help to the anticorruption body in each of its main fields of operation – enforcement, prevention and public education – and in general policy and staffing matters.

An effective way of achieving that objective has been found in the use of advisory committees of citizens. The anticorruption body therefore should have five advisory committees of citizens selected for their experience and expertise. They should comprise citizens appointed in their own right (not as representatives of any institution or organisation) and certain members of the public service appointed by reason of the office they hold. How these committees are appointed and how they work in practice, their size, function, composition, qualities of the members, their terms of appointment, selection, method of working and cost are set out briefly here. Initially these committees should be chaired by the head of the anticorruption body or his deputy until they have settled into a regular *modus operandi*.[1]

1 The initial period would vary from one committee to another but should be from one to three years.

It would be a mark of the importance attached to service on these committees if the appointments were made by the head of state, who would also select the members of the two advisory committees on policy and staff discipline. He would appoint members of the three operational committees from nominations put forward by the head of the anticorruption body since the body itself is the best judge of the operational assistance needed.

While the anticorruption body remains responsible for making the decisions, it is greatly assisted in the different aspects of its work by advice from these committees. The committees have a number of advantages. First, at general policy level a small group of prominent members of the community, meeting regularly with the head of the anticorruption body, provides advice on the shape and direction of the campaign against corruption and on personnel employment matters. Second, respected and respectable citizens with relevant experience voluntarily provide valuable advice on specialised topics for each arm of the strategy. Third, the committee considering complaints from the public on the conduct of officers provides independent consideration of the complaint and advice on disciplinary measures. Fourth, all these committees represent the community, demonstrate community involvement and, most importantly, monitor the conduct of the anticorruption body on behalf of the community.

Since public support in the fight against corruption is vital, this form of public involvement is key to developing the community's trust that builds active support. In particular, the committee working with the investigation department, as its main function, has to advise the head of the anticorruption body whether an investigation that cannot become a court case should be closed. As stated earlier, the great majority of investigations do not end up in court, either because the informant's suspicions were mistaken or because there is no sufficient evidence. It is vitally important that the public should have confidence that the allegation has been thoroughly investigated and that the matter can properly be closed. On behalf of the public this committee considers a report of the investigation and the recommendation by the investigating officers that no further action should be taken by the anticorruption body. It decides whether to advise acceptance of the recommendation. This committee's other job is to monitor the progress of investigations to see that they proceed with all reasonable speed. Obviously it is in this committee that a high degree of confidentiality is necessary.

Unpaid service to the community is certainly not rare in most countries and there is no doubt about its advantages. It appeals to people who are committed to the cause and who are prepared to donate their time and expertise to the general good. It saves taxpayers' money and it limits the amount of service that can properly be asked of anyone.

Members should be asked to serve for a period of twelve months, renewable if desired. They are appointed in a way that recognises the status of the position and their standing in the community. That is why the head of state should be invited to appoint them. Their appointment should be suitably publicised. They should not be overburdened, preparing for and attending a 2–3 hour meeting once a month being the maximum that should be asked of any of them. Though unpaid, they should be reimbursed the cost of travelling to and from meetings.

Advisory committees should be serviced by staff of the anticorruption body, who should be responsible for meeting schedules, agendas, circulation of material in advance and minutes of meetings. Meeting dates should be fixed twelve months in advance so that committee members can incorporate them into their busy schedules. Draft reports and recommendations should seek the specific advice of members. Meetings are kept as short as possible and occur no more often than once a month so as not to overburden committee members. Each committee reports annually to the head of state separately from the anticorruption body itself.

Community Support

Experience over many years has shown that advisory committees can be a most valuable support to the anticorruption body and a vital means of developing and maintaining the trust of the community.

THE CONTINUING ROLE OF THE NATIONAL ADMINISTRATION

Having provided the initial impetus for the national fight against corruption, the administration's effort obviously cannot end there. It has to continue to provide its support in a number of ways.

1. The provision of necessary resources, year in, year out – a matter considered in the previous chapter.
2. The administration needs to make clear to all its ministries, departments and agencies that the anticorruption body is there to lead the fight and that they are all to work with it and under its guidance.
3. The administration should instruct all its ministries, departments and agencies, including the law enforcement agencies, that all allegations and reports of corruption are to be referred, without delay and uninvestigated, to the anticorruption body.
4. The larger ministries and agencies, on the advice of the anticorruption body, should each be required to form an internal anticorruption unit to work with the anticorruption body in developing its own prevention and education initiatives. In the case of smaller entities of the administration, the appointment of a liaison officer will provide the link to the anticorruption body. Both the anticorruption unit and the liaison officer should be directly answerable to the head of the ministry, department or agency concerned.
5. The administration should make use of the anticorruption body to provide an integrity rating service so that an integrity assessment can be made of candidates

for senior appointments and promotions in the public service.

6 The administration should ensure the rules governing the conduct of ministers and public service employees are observed.

7 It is the responsibility of the administration to ensure that the principle of supervisory accountability applies throughout the public service.

8 Given that cooperative effort between the administration and the anticorruption body is essential to success against corruption, the administration should encourage all its ministries, departments and agencies to seek the advice of the anticorruption body in preventing corruption and in educating their employees.

9 The administration should put in place a debarment system for preventing any entity from bidding for a government contract if it has been guilty of corruption.

10 The administration has a duty to ensure that corruption prevention recommendations from the anticorruption body are put into effect.

11 The administration can and should encourage the community to help it fight corruption in rural development.

12 In many democratic countries party political funding and the funding of electoral campaigns is a major source of corruption. The administration should consider how this aspect of the country's corruption problem might be tackled.

13 The system of immunity from criminal process is in some countries far wider than is justified in a country that is subject to the rule of law. It is incumbent on the administration to ensure that immunity from the criminal process is reviewed and adjusted if necessary so as to apply to the fewest categories of people in the least number of circumstances. Likewise, the rules for the lifting of immunity should be reviewed and simplified.

14 If the country's anticorruption efforts are taking effect, it is incumbent on the administration to broadcast that progress abroad if it wishes to attract foreign investment and improve its reputation.

The suggestion is sometimes made that the anticorruption body should post an officer, perhaps undercover, to the most corruption-prone entities of the administration to find instances of corruption. This course should not be adopted. Undercover operations have their place in an anticorruption body's work but they are delicate operations fraught with risks and should be confined to specific investigations. Even if he were not undercover, the officer would run the risk of being quickly isolated or compromised. Furthermore, such a posting would run counter to the development of the entity's ownership of its own anticorruption measures and, in particular, of the responsibility of its own personnel to report suspicions of corruption.

Investigating corruption is usually a delicate matter. Such investigations, especially in their early stages, are fragile in the sense that evidence can quickly evaporate before it has been secured. Frequently corruption investigations that have been started by inexpert supervisors in the suspect's organisation are referred to the anticorruption body in a state that precludes any proper outcome. These matters are best left to the specialists. That is why all ministries, departments and agencies should be required to refer all reports or suspicions of corruption uninvestigated to the anticorruption body.

As regards the integrity rating service mentioned earlier, it is perhaps obvious that the probity of the public service requires that only officers of integrity should be appointed and promoted. The anticorruption body has an important part to play in that process. From its accumulated intelligence database it should be able to provide for the administration an integrity rating assessment. Whenever a senior appointment or promotion in the public service is being considered, the appointing authority should be required to turn to the anticorruption body for an assessment of the candidate's integrity.

The administration should ensure that the public service abides by its own regulations on the conduct of its public officers. The management of the public sector needs to ensure that those for whom they are responsible know what is expected of them, that those expectations are to be complied with and that any deviations from those standards will be followed by disciplinary action. For example, do public officers make a declaration of assets as and when the law requires? Is there any general understanding in the public service of what is meant by a conflict of interests and what the public officer who finds himself in that position is supposed to do? Do public officers know how to react correctly for their own protection if they are offered a bribe? It is the responsibility of management to ensure that those for whom they are responsible understand these matters.

The regulations governing the conduct of public employees are usually difficult to access. They tend to be buried in a large volume of regulations dealing with many other matters besides conduct. The format hardly lends itself to being tucked into an inside pocket or kept in the top drawer of one's desk. The electronic version is often difficult to find on the government website. The administration should see to it that the rules governing conduct of public employees are extracted and summarised into a brief code of conduct. The code should be a tailored, handy leaflet containing only the essentials. One of the essentials would be practical advice on how to react correctly in situations where the public officer's integrity is at risk of being compromised. The leaflet would serve as both a readily accessible, quick reference guide and, for the public, a source of information on what standards of behaviour to expect from public officers.

Any asset declaration system applicable to ministers and public service employees should ensure that the system has as its sole objective the identification of actual or potential conflict between public duties and personal interests, that it is so designed as to be able to meet that objective and that it is scrupulously observed by all those to whom it applies.

The significance of the principle of supervisory accountability, which is normally found in the regulations governing the conduct of public service employees, is often overlooked. The principle has an important bearing on the fight against corruption. If an officer under his supervision is found to have acted corruptly by taking advantage of a system falling into the supervisor's area of responsibility, the supervisor runs the risk of being found wanting in his duties of supervision and management. If he should have known of the corrupt activity and should have known of the vulnerability of the system, the supervisor's ignorance is a matter of disciplinary censure. That is why the administration should ensure that the principle of supervisory accountability is applied throughout the public service.

As regards a contract-tendering debarment system, in many countries the tendering system for public contracts gives rise to corruption. Many countries have in place a system for excluding from tendering any company or individual previously convicted of corruption. Given the perceived extent of the problem, the administration, with the assistance of the public procurement regulatory bodies and the anticorruption body, should design and adopt a debarment system that would prevent convicted entities from tendering for public contracts.

When it comes to giving effect to the corruption prevention recommendations of the anticorruption body, it can happen that the concerned ministry, department or agency does not implement the recommendations. The anticorruption body has no way of getting the recommendation implemented except by persuasion. If that fails, the anticorruption body has no power to compel compliance. The only effective way of proceeding then is to bring hierarchical pressure to bear on the recalcitrant ministry or department. In the absence of a satisfactory reason why the recommendations should not be promptly implemented, the anticorruption body should report the matter to the administration, which in turn should hold the recalcitrant public entity accountable.

The inspection of rural development projects undertaken by local government in a large developing country is difficult to carry out. Site inspection services are often stretched beyond their capacity. Added to that is corruption in the inspection services themselves. Some countries have successfully applied a system of community inspection or monitoring. If the beneficiary community is given the specifications (in simplified form if necessary), it can see for itself whether the project standards are being met. The thickness of a road surface or the size of construction timbers can be observed by the untrained eye. The relevant ministries of the administration should consider adopting this system of community self-help.

The funding of political parties and electoral campaigns presents a corruption problem in many democratic countries. The ever-growing demand for funding is seen as a source of serious corruption. The problem includes the misuse of state resources by electoral candidates. Rarely is funding and expenditure properly regulated. The administration would make a major and direct contribution to the fight against corruption if it were to regulate the financing of political parties and electoral campaigns.

In some countries judges, prosecutors, elected representatives, ministers and even senior civil servants enjoy immunity from criminal process on the ground that they could otherwise not perform their official functions fearlessly and impartially. These countries also have a more or less elaborate system for lifting the immunity in certain circumstances. The result is often that the incumbent cannot be dealt with even for corruption in office. The administration has a clear duty to re-examine the extent of immunities and the procedures for lifting immunity to ensure that they extend no further than is strictly necessary in a country that lives by the rule of law.

Every country makes considerable effort to project its image abroad. It is important for the world to know that the country is taking its corruption problem seriously and is not complacent about its anticorruption achievements. It falls to the administration to use all the means at its disposal, including its representative offices abroad and their contacts with foreign chambers of commerce, to convey the effectiveness of its anticorruption efforts.

THE LEGISLATURE'S CONTRIBUTION

Having completed the initial tasks of enacting the legislation that established the anticorruption body, the legislature's continuing role in the fight against corruption comprises several elements.

First, it will normally have a monitoring role in examining the annual reports of the anticorruption body and its advisory committees and questioning the administration on the progress of the effort against corruption. In doing so, legislators should guard against inquiring into investigations that may be opened, are under way or have been closed. Given their role as representatives of the people, legislators find it difficult to refrain from questions they regard as being in the public interest. It is vital to the success of the fight against corruption that they should appreciate the wider public interest of confidentiality in the investigative work of the anticorruption body in matters that may not or will not reach the public domain of the criminal justice system.

Second, the legislature will consider and approve the funding of the anticorruption effort through the national budgetary process.

Third, legislators and other elected representatives, like most citizens, will not always understand their personal duty when they find themselves in a situation that creates a conflict between their official duty and the personal interests of themselves or others. It is incumbent on them to gain a clear understanding of the concept of conflict of interests and their personal obligation in such situations. They should ensure that their house rules on the matter of declaring a personal interest are unambiguous and carry effective sanctions when they are broken. The speaker of the national assembly and chairmen of local councils should ensure that, with the help of the anticorruption body, members take part regularly in refresher courses on the matter.

Fourth, just as an asset declaration system applicable to ministers and public service employees should ensure that the system has as its sole objective the identification of actual or potential conflict between public duties and personal interests, so too an asset declaration system for elected representatives should have the same objective. There is a widespread misconception that the objective of a declaration of assets system is to identify the corrupt. It does no such thing. In the case of elected representatives, the system enables the public to know that when a representative speaks or votes on a matter, his personal interests may be affecting his stance. If the public is to be able to identify such a conflict of interest, it is necessary that the asset declaration be accessible to the public. It is for the legislature or the local assembly itself to establish a system that allows asset declarations to be publicly accessible as far as is necessary to fulfil the objective of identifying conflict of interests.

In many countries attempts to introduce a declaration of assets system for elected representatives have failed, either because the system has never been put in place or because the rules have been honoured more in the breach than the observance by members themselves. The message thus given to the community heightens the perception that corruption is growing even among the political leadership. A refusal to declare one's assets is taken to mean that one has ill-gotten gains to hide. If there is nothing to hide, why not declare, goes this line of thinking. Yet revealing substantial assets results in the inference that they are ill-gotten. The widespread misconception referred to earlier that the objective of the system is to identify the corrupt is largely responsible. The reluctance of elected representatives to subscribe to a declaration system designed on that basis is understandable. The inference that would inevitably be drawn by disclosing that one had substantial assets would prove nothing and would be unjust. The infringement of the right to privacy enshrined in the Constitution would be unjustifiable as being an unnecessarily wide derogation from that right. The size of one's savings account, for instance, would normally be irrelevant to any question of conflict of interests.

While these objections by elected representatives to such a system have merit, there is no denying that their refusal creates a poor impression in the community and in some countries has held up accession to the UN Convention Against Corruption. In such cases it is time to return to the drawing board and, with the assistance of the anticorruption body, to draft a declaration system based squarely and solely on the object of identifying any conflict of interests when an elected or appointed representative speaks or votes on a matter at hand. The design of a system based on that objective would take into account the content of the declaration and the extent to which the declaration needs to be made publicly available.

Fifth, the regulation of the funding of political parties and electoral campaigns referred to earlier is obviously a subject of direct concern to members of the legislature. They will no doubt have much say in shaping the regulating legislation.

Sixth, if elected representatives enjoy immunity from criminal process, especially as regards corruption, they have a duty to support the anticorruption effort by cooperating with the administration in reviewing the system of immunities.

Finally, in respect of their most obvious function as legislators, members of the lawmaking body should be aware of the opportunities for corruption created by the legislation they are about to enact. Not all those opportunities can always be avoided but legislators would be wise to call on the advice of the anticorruption body's prevention specialists while the draft can still be changed.

THE JUDICIARY'S CONTRIBUTION

Apart from the obvious duty of trying and sanctioning corrupt conduct, the judiciary has a number of contributions to make in fighting corruption.

As regards judiciary codes of conduct, judges, magistrates, presiding officers and court staff have ethical questions to resolve that do not necessarily arise in the duties of other public officials. The codes of conduct that apply to the judiciary therefore have significant differences from the general code applicable to all public servants. Like other public servants, however, judges, magistrates and their staff need practical guidance on how to react correctly and for their own protection when improperly approached. The head of the judiciary should ensure that its codes of conduct are, with the assistance of the anticorruption body, reviewed, promulgated, observed and enforced.

The earlier observation that senior people should not always be assumed to be knowledgeable about the notion of conflict of interests applies equally to the judiciary. The head of the judiciary should arrange to have instituted a regular programme of promoting a thorough understanding among the judiciary, including presiding officers and senior court staff, of the concept of conflict of interests and of the personal responsibility that rests on the individual. Again, the anticorruption body's assistance would be helpful.

Any declaration of assets system adopted for judges and magistrates should, as any such system, be based on the objective of identifying conflict of interests. That objective governs the architecture of the system. Declarations should therefore be seen by the senior judge in charge of allocating the court's business.

If judges and prosecutors enjoy immunity from criminal process, especially as regards corruption, they – like elected representatives – have a duty to support the anticorruption effort by cooperating with the administration in reviewing the system of immunities applicable to them.

The success of the national fight against corruption depends upon the effective enforcement of the laws against corruption. In turn, effective enforcement largely depends on minimum delay in the matter reaching trial. A climate of over-tolerance of applications for postponements is a major factor in the delay of cases coming on for trial. Senior judges have an important role to play in conveying and reinforcing that message to the rest of the judiciary.

Corruption cases could be given priority over other cases, which would mean a corruption case going to the top of the waiting list as soon as it was registered at the court. That could have the undesirable result of a minor corruption case leapfrogging more serious cases of other criminality. A mechanism could be devised to address this problem: a magistrate would consider an application by the prosecutor to move the corruption case to the top of the list. He would be able to weigh the importance of getting the corruption case dealt with against the nature and seriousness of the cases listed ahead of it. The endorsement of the head of the judiciary for such a system would ensure its adoption.

Special courts within the normal court system could be designated to deal with corruption cases. These courts would provide a forum for the speedy disposal of corruption cases and would develop an expertise allowing them to deal with such cases more efficiently. In the absence of corruption cases the court would deal with other cases. Again, the endorsement of the head of the judiciary and the support of his judges for creating such a court would ensure its adoption.

In many developing countries customary courts deal with relatively minor offences at local district level. These courts are usually the most numerous and are spread throughout the country. They provide the closest contact with the justice system that the citizen will normally have. Justice is dispensed summarily and swiftly, there is usually no backlog of cases and the accused has the right to be tried in a higher court if he wishes. And again, the support of the senior judiciary for the use of these courts would carry great weight. The active encouragement of their use in appropriate cases could have a profound effect on the problem of delay.

A system of cautioning offenders in minor cases could be used. Given the anticorruption body's essential policy of investigating with a view to prosecution every allegation of corruption capable of being investigated, it is inevitable that many of their cases will be trivial instances of bribery. These cases contribute to the backlog of cases in the courts. In several countries there exists for appropriately minor criminal cases a system of formally cautioning the offender without taking him to court. The matter is disposed of by a formal caution administered by a senior officer and the caution is noted on the offender's record. Certain preconditions would apply: the matter was trivial, the suspect admitted the offence, the suspect had not previously been cautioned for a similar offence and the prosecutor had given prior agreement to the matter being dealt with by way of caution. Additionally the number of such disposals would be included in the statistics contained in the anticorruption body's annual report.

A specialised unit in the public prosecutor's office to deal with corruption cases should be considered. The obvious advantage of such a unit acquiring an expertise in handling corruption cases is the resulting speed and efficiency. Given the importance of processing corruption cases rapidly, a specialised prosecution unit would provide an important support to the national anticorruption effort.

INVOLVING THE BUSINESS SECTOR

The ethical dilemmas of the private sector differ considerably from one part of that sector to another. The ethical questions of the financial sector are not those of the construction industry or the retail trades. One code of conduct cannot apply to all. The private sector umbrella organisations and the anticorruption body should together assist each part of this sector to prepare a model code of conduct for adoption by enterprises within that part of the sector.

The role of the private sector in affecting the community's attitude to corruption can hardly be overstated. It is therefore crucially important that the representative organisations of the business sector should join in partnership with the anticorruption body in promoting ethical conduct in business. Small and medium enterprises in particular, which lack the resources for an in-house corporate compliance unit, need help. Experience shows that an ethics resource centre can provide that help efficiently and cheaply. A partnership with the anticorruption body, making use of one of its centrally placed branch premises and of its personnel to man the centre, allows the centre to be run by a board of business people which sets the centre's policy and directs its activities.

Promoting sectoral model codes of conduct, providing advice to business companies and helping the anticorruption body spread the anticorruption message throughout the private sector have been demonstrated to improve the climate for doing business.

Since the investigation of corruption depends on information from the public, private sector employees are an essential source of information on corruption in both the public and private sectors. The private sector's umbrella organisations can have a positive effect in influencing employers to encourage employees to report corruption and to ensure protection from subsequent discrimination. The umbrella organisations, with the help of the anticorruption body, should mobilise their member enterprises for a 'report corruption without fear' campaign, emphasising that all reports to the anticorruption body are made in strict confidence.

COMMUNITY PARTICIPATION

The professions, the trade unions, the community-based organisations like sports associations, the religious bodies and the non-governmental organisations have an active part to play in the same way as described for the private sector in the preceding paragraphs. The anticorruption body should help them develop model codes of conduct. They should make a point of encouraging their members and adherents, as responsible citizens, to support the fight against corruption by reporting suspicions of corruption to the anticorruption body.

CONCLUDING REMARKS

In recognising that public support is one of the essentials for beating corruption, we must also realise that that support will not spring up overnight. Overcoming resignation, apathy and fear can be a slow process. Yet it must be done. Trust in the anticorruption body and active support of its leadership in fighting corruption must be developed methodically and continuously. It is equally important to realise that community trust is fragile; it can be lost overnight. That thought has proved to be the strongest incentive for proper conduct by the officers of the anticorruption body.

9
Endurance

INTRODUCTION

This, the seventh and final essential for success against corruption, should come as no surprise. When corruption has for a long time infected every part of the daily life of a community, there is unlikely to be a miraculous overnight cure. The treatment is likely to be long and painful. We need to find the stamina, we need endurance.

But, if we are to undergo the treatment, we need to know how long it will last, that the cost will be manageable, that the pain can be assuaged, that we will see signs of progress, that the chances of a successful cure are good if we stick to the treatment. In this chapter these aspects of the fight against corruption are considered. Finally, the question is put: did the success of the treatment make it worth undergoing?

THE TIME THAT IT TAKES

Looking around the world today at the projects and programmes designed to deal with corruption, one could be forgiven for thinking that the problem is to be solved within the life of the project or programme. That is unrealistic, but the question must be asked: how long will it take?

If the question means: how long before we can say that corruption no longer undermines our development, that we as a community have transformed ourselves from being tolerant, apathetic, resigned to corruption as part of our daily lives to being unwilling to accept, refusing to allow, willing to fight corruption and prevent it taking hold, how long does it take for that transformation to take place, the reply is: less than a generation, less than twenty years. A long time some may think, but no time at all in the historical development of a nation. That does not mean that nothing happens until suddenly the transformation occurs. It is a gradual process, and the progress can be seen from the beginning. Measuring that progress is referred to later in this chapter.

ASSUAGING THE PAIN

Fighting corruption is a test of a community's endurance. And tests of endurance involve pain. If our will to fight is to hold, we should see what can be done to ease the pain. Chapter 3 dealt with political will to undertake the fight. It will be recalled that the pain of the past and how to deal with it was discussed. The various options for freeing ourselves of the burden of past corruption were examined.

The best solution suggested was a general amnesty with an exception for past conduct that was simply too heinous to be overlooked. An allegation judged to fall into the heinous category would be investigated in the normal way. Otherwise conduct occurring before a certain date would not be investigated by the anticorruption body. For a community long plagued by corruption, a general amnesty would be a powerful analgesic. The relief from pain would be enormous.

The fight against corruption should take care not to impose more pain than the community can endure. That is why the anticorruption body should investigate only what the community comes to complain about. There are some matters the community is not yet ready to complain about for fear of the consequences. There will come a time when it will, but not just yet. One of the reasons underlying the investigating policy of the anticorruption body – that it investigates every allegation brought to it and, as a corollary, does not initiate its own investigations – is that in that way the anticorruption body shows itself to be responsive to the wishes of the community and does not go barging in where it is not yet wanted. The community itself is the best judge of how much pain it can take.

A third way in which a community assuages the pain of fighting corruption is in the sanctioning of corrupt conduct. It is evident that corrupt conduct can vary from the heinous to the morally venial. The sanction that the courts will apply will therefore vary according to the circumstances of the particular case. The state school teacher who each day asks for and accepts a little something from her pupils to supplement her salary is not to be treated as severely as the multi-million dollar fraudster who has bribed the bank manager. That is why our judges must be given the discretion to deal appropriately with those found guilty of corruption and why minimum sentences will always be unduly harsh and unjust in certain cases. Punishment unjustly inflicted and causing unmerited pain will be self-defeating.

TURNING THE CORNER

Although some pain is inevitable, it will be more than compensated for when the results begin to show, when the country's revenue streams begin to flow again into the treasury, when citizens begin to realise that things can be different, that the cost of corruption does not have to be part of the cost of living or of doing business. When he senses that his personal attitude to corruption and that of his friends is changing for the better, he and his community are justified in thinking that real progress is being made.

MEASURING PROGRESS

Measuring that progress now needs considering. It is necessary that the community, including the government and the taxpayer, should be able to gauge progress. The will to fight on is sustained by visible signs of progress. Nothing succeeds like success, particularly in the fight against corruption where success in any of the three elements of the strategy strengthens the other two. That mutual reinforcement is the reason why the strategy has proved successful.

How then should progress be measured? Essentially there are two ways, each of which complements the other: operational statistical data on one hand and statistics on community perception and attitude on the other. The operational statistics concern the daily work of the anticorruption body in carrying out its mandate and are collected and collated by the anticorruption body itself. Statistics on community perceptions and attitudes are measured most accurately by public opinion surveys carried out independently of the anticorruption body.

THE STATISTICAL PICTURE

The operational statistics should relate to each of the three elements of the strategy – enforcement, prevention and public education and support. The statistics obtained from the public opinion survey should relate to people's perception of the incidence of corruption, people's support for the fight against corruption and people's personal attitude towards corruption. The types of data required are set out here to indicate the statistical picture that should emerge.

Enforcement

Number of corruption reports
Number of identified reports/anonymous reports
Number of pursuable reports
Number of non-corruption reports referred to other agencies
Number of investigations started
Number of investigations completed
Number of prosecutions
Number of convictions
Value of assets recovered and forfeited to the state
Public perceptions of incidence of corruption
Public perceptions of effectiveness of investigation and prosecution

Prevention – Systems Enhancement

Number of systems examined
Number of recommendations made
Number of recommendations adopted
Number of system changes subsequently evaluated
Client perception of value of system changes
Perceptions of quality of service delivery in systems examined

Prevention – Community Relations (public education and support)

Number of anti-corruption talks given
Number of people, by sector, reached through talks
Number of teaching institutions visited
Number of teaching institutions adopting anti-corruption ethics in curriculum
Number of public service departments and agencies allowing staff to attend talks
Number of government agencies adopting anti-corruption code of conduct
Number of private sector companies contacted and addressed
Number of companies adopting codes of conduct
Number of electronic media 'slots' and items of public information
Number of print media advertisements, feature articles, news items
Coverage achieved by media campaigns and poster campaigns
Change in public perceptions of incidence of corruption
Change in awareness of corruption issues
Change in personal attitudes to corruption
Change in awareness of, respect for and trust in the anticorruption body

It will be apparent from what has gone before that it is the last four of these measurements that are the most important. In particular, change in personal attitude to corruption is the indicator showing that the ultimate objective of the fight against corruption is achievable. The last indicator, trust in the anticorruption body, is crucial for developing public support, one of the essentials without which no campaign against corruption can succeed.

GAUGING PUBLIC OPINION

A little more should now be said about the survey of public opinion. The regular measurement of public opinion should be commissioned by the anticorruption body and professionally carried out by an independent firm. The survey should measure the public's perception of the corruption situation in the country, the public's regard for the anticorruption body and, most importantly, people's personal attitude to corruption. It is the community's individual attitude of resistance to corruption that is the mark of true progress in the fight against corruption.

The objective of a public opinion survey is twofold: first, the survey result serves as a management tool enabling the anticorruption body to adjust the implementation of the strategy from year to year; second, the first survey provides a benchmark against which to measure progress by comparing the results of subsequent surveys. It should therefore be done at the outset, even if the picture revealed looks bleak – later snapshots can only be better!

For the sake of independence, impartiality and credibility, it should not be done by the anticorruption body itself but should be commissioned. However, the anticorruption body must ensure that the questions asked include those required for its own purposes. Subsequent surveys should ask the same questions of the same population sample if a valid comparison is to be made, if progress over time is to be shown.

PUBLICISING PROGRESS

It follows that the survey results should be made public. Taken with the operational statistical picture, the community is thus able to see what progress is being made. Without that picture the community is unlikely to want to continue investing its time, energy and taxpayers' hard-earned money. And as progress becomes apparent, so the momentum builds. Before long, a community that had all but resigned itself to corruption finds that it is getting the upper hand and can sense victory.

STAYING ON TOP

Now a word of caution. No modern state that has curbed corruption has been able to dismantle its anticorruption defences.

If the community relaxes its grip on the problem, it tends quickly to return. The reality therefore is that the fight against corruption continues into the foreseeable future. Perhaps to the chagrin of the minister of finance, the fight against corruption will always be a line item of the government's annual budget.

WORTH THE EFFORT?

Let us turn finally to the question posed at the beginning of this chapter: did the success of the treatment make it worth undergoing? Much research has been done by institutions like the World Bank on the cost of corruption and the economic benefits that flow from defeating this curse. What is gained in terms of social trust and cohesion is perhaps more difficult to calculate. How to calculate the moral wellbeing of a community is no doubt a difficult subject. Is the happiness quotient higher without corruption in our lives? Most people intuitively would say yes. And perhaps that is enough. Anecdotally, if one were to ask the citizens of places that are recognised as having got on top of corruption (Singapore, Hong Kong) whether is was worth spending those hard-earned tax dollars to get there, the question would be regarded as odd. The reply would be that the cost was the best investment that they had ever made. The businessmen of Hong Kong, not often considered tender sentimentalists, would tell you that they could not have built Hong Kong as they have done if Hong Kong still had the corruption that it had forty years ago.

The vision of a life without corruption explains why so often governments are elected when they have promised they will deal with corruption. That they so often fail to deliver is the reason for this little book.

It must, however, also be said that, even when an administration starts its anticorruption journey down the right road, there are numerous pitfalls on the way, any one of which can spell disaster. The final chapter summarily describes some of the more usual pitfalls and how to avoid them.

10
Pitfalls of Fighting Corruption

INTRODUCTION

Nobody has ever said that tackling corruption is easy. The world is strewn with the wrecks of anticorruption efforts. In modern times success has proved elusive; success stories are scarce. The World Bank acknowledges that in the last decade or so that it has been concentrating considerable effort on the problem of corruption, progress has been disappointing.

The experience of so many failures should not, however, go to waste. There is as much to be learned from the failures as from the few successes. This chapter[1] lists briefly what can go wrong and goes on to list, equally briefly, how to get things right.

Anticorruption initiatives are usually created when corruption has spread so widely and the police are so corrupt that offences of bribery are no longer investigated or prosecuted. In a desperate attempt to stop the rot the government establishes an anticorruption agency, half believing that the problem will then disappear. New laws, new corruption offences, more severe penalties, a new agency but still the problem gets worse. Many of these initiatives fail dismally to have any impact. Very few can be said to have succeeded at all. Why?

SOME OF THE THINGS THAT GO WRONG

The causes of failure fall into broad categories relating to political considerations, realism in objectives and expectations,

1 It is based on a paper requested for an experts' meeting of a UN agency's Global Programme Against Corruption held in Vienna in April 2000.

strategic vision, the anticorruption laws, implementation policies and practices, public confidence and staying in control of the problem.

Weak political will Even if the determination to tackle corruption was initially strong (usually from a government newly in power) it often diminishes as the realities of office, the vested interests in the status quo and the pressure of more immediate tasks bear on the actions of government.

Lack of resources The anticorruption initiative competes with other even more demanding causes for the limited financial and personnel resources available. Without adequate resources the anticorruption agency cannot do its job.

Political interference Well-intentioned but overly-detailed monitoring of the operational activities of the agency leads to ineffectiveness. Sometimes the interference is deliberately intended to aim the agency at political opponents who therefore have every interest in hampering its work. Sometimes the interference is done through an instinct of self-preservation.

Fear of consequences Often related to self-preservation, fear of the pain caused by effective enforcement drives the government to curb the agency's operations.

Non-belief in benefits A reluctance to accept that real benefits will accrue – economic, social, administrative and political – leads to questioning whether the painful effort is worthwhile.

Unrealistic aim and expectations The erroneous belief that corruption can be eradicated and the expectation that it can be achieved in a short time are inevitably disappointed and result in discouragement.

Traditional reliance on enforcement alone The understandable reaction to the extensive criminality of corruption is the enactment of more offences, severer penalties and stronger investigative powers that erode human rights, ignoring the numerous lessons of experience that enforcement alone never deals with corruption but on the contrary tends to make matters worse.

Failure to understand nature of corruption The mistake of relying on enforcement is the result of failing to understand the nature of corruption, that it is secretive and complicitous, that it is not a crime that leaves an aggrieved 'victim' in the usual sense who is likely to provide information about the crime and give evidence in court, and that anyway people often do not see it as a crime and so are unlikely to be concerned to help the authorities. In addition, people have only a vague idea of the harm caused by corruption – the causal connection between corruption and many of the ills of society is difficult to see.

Governance reform mistaken for anticorruption In many countries the belief has been fostered that corruption can be defeated by governance reform. There is a failure to realise that every attempted governance reform fails to take root because it is undermined by the pre-existing corruption. That failure stems from a lack of understanding of the conceptual difference between governance and anticorruption, governance being about running things, anticorruption being about upholding certain values.

Lack of strategy Failure to understand the nature of corruption makes policymakers fail to realise that corruption cannot be dealt with by enforcement alone, as one might deal with burglary or rape. Countries try to deal with corruption by investigating, prosecuting and sentencing, but they do not try to prevent corruption by eliminating the opportunities for behaving corruptly nor do they try to change people's attitude to corruption.

Inadequate law Often the laws against corruption are inadequate in that they are either overly complicated and unintelligible or they do not contain some basic offences. For example, the law applies only to public officials and not to the private sector, or only to the receiver of a bribe and not the giver, or does not prohibit public officials from soliciting or receiving gifts – gifts that cannot be proved to be an inducement or reward. Sometimes the law is created as an elaborate instrument aimed at the wrong objective. An example is the system of declarations of assets that legislators and public officials are required to make. Sometimes the problem lies in weak investigative powers and inadequate evidential provisions with the result that corruption offences cannot be prosecuted effectively.

Lack of coordination Even when a country recognises that fighting corruption requires more than merely enforcing the laws and has a strategy involving the elements of prevention and public education, the strategy fails because its elements are not advanced together, are not coordinated and thus fail to reinforce each other.

Lack of focus, not sole function Fighting corruption is sometimes made the responsibility of a body which already has other functions. The Auditor General or the Comptroller General, the Ombudsman, the Commissioner for Human Rights and even the State Revenue Service have all been pressed into service. Not surprisingly, the fight against corruption is not and cannot be the most important item in their portfolios.

Given the wrong responsibility Sometimes an anticorruption agency is created but is given additional responsibilities that distract it from its main function. Examples are the policing of election regulations, not merely electoral bribery, 'economic crime', 'misappropriation of public funds', 'embezzlement', 'fraud' and 'moneylaundering'. In recent years governance reforms have often been made the responsibility of the anticorruption body.

Not given sole responsibility A common mistake is to fail to make the anticorruption agency the only body responsible for investigating corruption allegations. Instead of channelling all such allegations in one direction, other agencies are expected to take a hand – the police, the audit department, the revenue services, even the public service administration. The result is usually incompetent investigation half-heartedly done.

Overwhelmed by the past The past is especially a problem in countries that have suffered widespread corruption for many years. The government announces a new initiative and launches an anticorruption agency that will deal with the problem. Public expectation is raised. The agency opens its doors for business. Two things can happen. Either the new agency is swamped by information from the public that it cannot properly deal with, much of it going back years. For want of time and resources current corruption goes unchecked. Alternatively resentment from influential sectors of the community builds up against the effective action taken on past misdeeds and the political will to continue the fight fades.

Minimal community involvement If little has been done to involve the community in the work of the agency, the inevitable result is that the public comes to distrust the agency and provides no information about what is going on. Without that information the agency's investigative powers are useless. Furthermore, its preventive and educational work is likely to be ignored. There is another problem that results: the community tends to sit back and leave the entire fight to the anticorruption agency, believing that, having brought the agency into being, there is nothing else to do but leave it to cope as best it can.

Lack of transparency Some of the fight against corruption requires confidentiality if it is to be effective. Strong investigative powers are needed. But the combination of strong powers and confidentiality easily breeds suspicion in the public mind that the agency is abusing its position. Without a conscious effort to open up to public scrutiny in those areas of its work where it can do so, the agency grows secretive. Only exceptionally can it then remain effective.

Insufficient accountability Any government body in receipt of public funds should be required to account for the way it has spent that money. An anticorruption agency which regards itself as an exception is doomed to fail. Failure to account for its implementation of the strategy and for the conduct of its officers will alienate the public. Without community support it cannot do its job.

Confidentiality not preserved Informants are usually reluctant or fearful. The source of information dries up if confidentiality is not assured or even if the informant is required to identify himself before his complaint can be investigated.

Selectivity in investigations Anticorruption agencies are often tempted to be selective in the allegations they investigate, if only from an understandable desire to prioritise in order to stretch scarce resources to maximum effect. If they do so, they almost certainly lose public support. First, putting aside a minor allegation will deter the complainant from returning, perhaps with a much more important matter. Second, what appears minor quite often turns out to be important when investigated. Third, picking and choosing what to investigate and what not to investigate raises suspicions of improper motives, if not of corruption. Fourth, selecting what to investigate sends out the message that some corruption does not matter, that double standards apply. Fifth, numerous small acts of corruption are detrimental to the well-being of a country, and even a trivial act of corruption can have catastrophic consequences. They all contribute to loss of public confidence in the agency.

Failure to develop public trust Anticorruption agencies are often established at a time when the public is sceptical, distrustful or even hostile about state institutions. Yet time and again these agencies do little to develop public trust. Often they are unaware of the vital need to do so.

Lack of strict code of values and discipline In an atmosphere of pervasive corruption it is easy for the agency's staff to live and work and behave no differently from the rest of the community. No particular code of conduct is made to apply to them, no discipline prevails, no disciplinary action is taken. Those appointed to uphold the values set out in the law are no different from the rest of the community.

Loss of morale In such an atmosphere it is hardly surprising that the morale of the staff of the agency sinks. There is no pride in the institution or in the job.

Agency itself becomes corrupt Before long corruption begins to spread in the agency itself. When that happens, it only remains to bury that particular anticorruption initiative, the sooner the better.

WHAT'S TO BE DONE?

From what has been described so far, what needs to be done to give the next anticorruption initiative a chance of success should be obvious. The lessons are there to be applied next time.

Back to the drawing board Assuming that the situation in the country has not improved and that the police are as corrupt as ever, the first thing to be done is to return to the drawing board and rethink the problem and its solution.

National strategy, clear, comprehensive and coherent Having realised that corruption is a complex phenomenon, the conclusion should follow that fighting it requires a strategy – clear, coherent and comprehensive. It is now recognised that the strategy must comprise three elements:

1. The laws enshrining our community values on corruption must be enforced, of course.
2. Corruption must be prevented by eliminating from the systems in which we work and live the opportunities for corruption.
3. We must educate everyone about corruption and we must involve the community and get people to join the fight.

Coordination The strategy has to be given every chance to succeed. We know that if its three elements are advanced together from the beginning they are a stronger force than if each element acts separately. So their implementation must be coordinated. A person or body will have to do that job of coordination. And if the reasons for failing the first time included the fact that the elements were entrusted to different agencies which lacked dedication to the task, the job of coordinating and implementing the strategy will have to be made the responsibility of one agency – one agency dedicated to fighting corruption and given no other tasks that might detract from its central duty.

Governance and anticorruption distinguished This time the conceptual difference between governance and anticorruption will be kept constantly in mind: governance is about running things, anticorruption is about upholding cerain values. Governance reform will not be the responsibility of the anticorruption agency but will be undertaken by a separate part of the administration.

Improved laws – offences, investigative powers, evidentiary provisions A review of the anticorruption laws will have to be carried out and changes made where necessary. The objective is to have clear, basic offences, adequate penalties, strong investigative powers and evidentiary provisions in aid of successful prosecution.

An independent and accountable agency The agency will be created by law. The law will both provide for its independence and specify the methods by which it is to be accountable to the community. It will also provide for the agency to be properly resourced from public funds voted by the legislature. It will provide for the appointment and removal of the head of the agency and make the agency responsible for coordinating and implementing the strategy. The head of the agency will be the appointing and disciplinary authority for the staff.

Proper selection of personnel The agency cannot afford to have working for it anyone whose integrity is in doubt. Ability and dedication are not enough. A selection procedure that includes positive checking is therefore essential.

Decent terms of employment For most of the personnel second jobs to supplement public service salaries will not be permissible. So agency staff must be paid enough for a decent standard of living and be provided with adequate working conditions. Staff will be employed on renewable contract terms with an end-of-contract gratuity. Recruits from the civil service will have the right, for a limited period, to return to the civil service.

Code of conduct and discipline If agency staff are to be treated as an elite corps, they must behave accordingly. They must know from the beginning that they will be expected to conduct themselves to a high standard. They must also know that their conduct will be monitored and that lapses of discipline will not be overlooked. Serious misconduct or questionable integrity will lead to dismissal by their disciplinary authority, the head of the agency.

Community involvement The most serious mistake made the first time will not be repeated. The government now knows it cannot take on corruption without community support. This time the community will be involved from the outset. First, in proposing ways in which the strategy is to be implemented. Second, in serving on advisory committees that will offer guidance to the agency on developing each element of the strategy and, as representatives of the community, monitor the way the agency does its job. Third, the leaders of every part of the community will be enlisted to take the message to their own people and get them on side.

Accountability Proper accounts audited by the public auditor, an annual report to the executive and the legislature, and answerability for the conduct of subordinates will all be features of the new agency. The advisory committees will report separately.

Transparency Confidentiality will be kept to the minimum necessary to do the job properly. Everything that can be made public will be. Consistently with that policy, inquiries from the press and the public will be dealt with promptly and accurately.

Confidentiality Where confidentiality is necessary, everything will be done to maintain it and to make that clear to the public.

A fresh start This time the leadership of the country will consider the advantages and risks of making a break from the past and starting afresh. It is a decision that can be taken only at the top. But it will be taken at the outset and, whatever the decision, it will be explained to the people.

Adequate funding Knowing now that corruption cannot be fought effectively without an investment of scarce national resources, the political resolve will keep this national problem on the agenda and be translated into voted public funds.

Lessons from elsewhere Those responsible for implementing the strategy will be alert to the lessons to be learned from other countries, both their mistakes and their successes. Anything that could improve the chances of success should be heeded.

Leadership The simple but highly effective lesson of leadership by example will be encouraged at every level, the example from the very top being the most effective.

Benchmarks for measuring achievements This time the agency will keep figures of what it does and will publish them. The public will be regularly sounded out, not only about what it thinks of the corruption situation in the country and of the agency itself, but more importantly what the individual's own attitude is to corruption. Over time the extent of true success, the change of personal attitude to corruption, will be tracked in these surveys.

Realisation that beating corruption takes time and resources This time the policymakers and legislators know that the battle cannot be won in a day. They know it will take time and resources. Yet they also know the rewards of success are worth the investment. And once on top of corruption, the country will have to stay on top. That means that fighting corruption becomes a permanent item of public expenditure.

Chances of success? Despite the lessons learned and applied, the new, better anticorruption agency cannot guarantee success. Anything could go wrong, but the prospects of the agency making a real contribution to winning the battle are considerably brighter.

CLOSING REMARKS

This list of things that go wrong and things that could be put right is not comprehensive. No doubt other reasons could be advanced why so many national anticorruption strategies and anticorruption agencies are ineffective. And it must be emphasised that an anticorruption agency is not in itself the answer to a beleaguered country's corruption problems. An agency can ever only be a part of the solution. But it is the part on which success depends.